Magic and the Magician

❖❖❖❖❖❖❖❖❖❖❖❖❖❖❖❖❖❖❖❖❖❖❖❖❖❖❖❖❖❖

E. NESBIT AND HER CHILDREN'S BOOKS

E. NESBIT AS A YOUNG WOMAN – 1887

Magic and the Magician

E. NESBIT AND HER CHILDREN'S BOOKS

By NOEL STREATFEILD

Abelard Schuman Limited *London New York Toronto*

© *Noel Streatfeild 1958*
Library of Congress Catalogue
Card Number 62-17795

London: Abelard-Schuman Limited, 8 King Street, WC2
New York: Abelard-Schuman Limited, 6 West 57 Street,
New York 19
Toronto: Abelard-Schuman Canada Limited, 896 Queens Street,
West Toronto 3

Printed in Great Britain

Contents

	Acknowledgements	9
ONE	E. Nesbit	11
TWO	School Days	21
THREE	Brighton and Buckinghamshire	31
FOUR	Fears	44
FIVE	France	52
SIX	Germany and Halstead	62
SEVEN	The Bastables	68
EIGHT	Oswald Bastable	82
NINE	Robert, Anthea, Jane, Cyril and the Lamb	90
TEN	The Psammead	101
ELEVEN	The Phoenix	110
TWELVE	'The Railway Children'	117
THIRTEEN	'The Enchanted Castle'	127
FOURTEEN	'The House of Arden' and 'Harding's Luck'	135
FIFTEEN	The Warps: Mouldi–Mouldier–Mouldiest	140
SIXTEEN	The Magician	151
	Book List	157

Illustrations

E. Nesbit as a young woman – 1887   *Frontispiece*

E. Nesbit aged three   *Facing page* 16

E. Nesbit with her Nurse   17

Sarah Nesbit – E. Nesbit's Mother   32

Well Hall – The Nesbits' House   33

'I don't suppose he was used to politeness from boys'   80

'The Uncle was very fierce indeed with the pudding'   81

'Poof, poof, poofy,' he said, and made a grab   96

'But there's only half of it there!'   97

'Try another verse,' said the Phoenix   112

Everyone helped – even the Phoenix   113

The engine-driver took the little engine and looked at it   122

A photograph from the B.B.C.'s Television Production of *The Railway Children*   123

She saw that fully half of the chairs were occupied, and by the Queerest people   134

The Mouldiwarp made a little run and a little jump   135

Acknowledgements

My most grateful thanks are due:

To E. Nesbit's daughter, Mrs. Philips, for telling me what her mother told her of her childhood.

To Mrs. Doris Langley Moore, E. Nesbit's first biographer, for providing the text of a number of autobiographical articles written by E. Nesbit for the now defunct periodical *The Girl's Own Paper*, which she discovered too late to use herself in her *E. Nesbit, a Biography*. My thanks are also due to her for permission to quote some of Noel Bastable's verse which I myself was unable to unearth, and for generous help and encouragement while I was writing this book.

To Mr. Noël Coward for permission to quote what he wrote to me about E. Nesbit.

To Miss Lily Streatfeild who was born only eight years after E. Nesbit, and who has therefore been able to give invaluable help in reconstructing the world in which E. Nesbit was brought up.

To the Proprietors of *Punch* for permission to reprint the verses on pages 155–6.

To Wells Gardner Darton & Co., Ltd., and the British Broadcasting Corporation for permission to reproduce the illustrations facing pages 122 and 123 respectively.

❖❖❖❖❖❖❖❖❖❖❖❖❖❖❖❖❖❖❖❖❖❖❖❖❖❖❖❖❖❖

CHAPTER ONE

E. Nesbit

❖❖❖❖❖❖❖❖❖❖❖❖❖❖❖❖❖❖❖❖❖❖❖❖❖❖❖❖❖❖

IN THE YEAR 1858 on the fifteenth of August a daughter was born to John and Sarah Nesbit. The child was christened Edith, though in the family circle she was called Daisy. But as a writer she is known to us simply as E. Nesbit.

The background and personality of a writer of adult fiction is not necessarily revealed in their books, but something of the background and personality of a good children's author is almost always discernible, for it is their ability to remember with all their senses their own childhood, and what it felt like to be a child, that makes their work outstanding. E. Nesbit, because she has been read and loved by many generations of children, has established herself as one of the great, and today her books are ranked as classics. What made them classics? What had she to give, that causes her books to be read and loved and sold widely a hundred years after her birth? What quality have they that eight of them, adapted as plays, have been broadcast on the Children's Hour so successfully that many of them have been repeated several times? By what magic was *The Railway Children* unaltered in plot, and using largely the original dialogue, able to become an immensely popular serial on television?

What makes E. Nesbit so fascinating a writer to

study is that her children's books, with one exception, are divorced from the life she lived as an adult, for they have their roots in her childhood, and a very early childhood at that. Reading what has been written about her, and told about her, by those who can remember her, it is almost impossible not to believe there were two Nesbits. In this book, which concerns itself with her childhood until about the age of thirteen, and with ten of her children's books, there are many quotations from articles written by herself about her childhood. In these we see the temperamental, deeply sensitive child, grow into a passionate, temperamental, would-be poet. That child she describes would seem to have nothing in common with the Nesbit The Fabian Society knew, that Wells wrote about in his *Experiment in Autobiography*, the Nesbit who was a byword as a bohemian hostess, whose charm, wit, gaiety, and almost frightening temperament surrounded her throughout her adult life, with those who admired her almost to the point of idolatry. Was it possible that the E. Nesbit the world knew was an invention of the real Nesbit's, built originally for an insecure, shy girl to hide behind, but into whose skin she grew, and out of which she only emerged when she was writing for children, and at the very end of her life? It is not unusual for those in need of support to build a façade behind which to hide, to accept that E. Nesbit was such a person makes E. Nesbit the writer for children wholly understandable.

In nearly all the Nesbit books for children there is a wealth of affection given to the house in which her families live. The house in which E. Nesbit was born is therefore of importance in understanding her, since it was the only permanent home the child was to know until she was thirteen. The house was in Kennington Lane, where her father was head of an agricultural college. In 1858 Kennington Lane was a residential area, not smart, but the Nesbits would have been surrounded by other comfortably off middle-class families. And how comfortable in many ways the middle classes of that period were. Those maids who function in almost all the Nesbit books, however low the family finances, undoubtedly have their roots in that house in Kennington Lane, where there was always a staff to run the house and look after the children.

E. Nesbit must have had *par excellence* that writer's gift of a blotting-paper memory, for though she was only to know Kennington Lane as a very small child, the influence not only of the house, but of the environment was to stay with her always. Although the Nesbits and their friends were most comfortably off, there was poverty round the corner, and very real poverty at that. It was not unlikely from figures of similar areas that over six thousand people in near-by streets could have been housed in fewer than seven hundred houses, and the squalor and stench would have been appalling. The Nesbit who wrote the children's books, except in *Harding's Luck*, kept her children strictly to the middle-class world to which they belonged, and their attitude to the lower classes was exactly what it would have been. But there are many small touches which show she had seen real poverty, and it must have been near Kennington Lane, for as later chapters will show, it was her only opportunity to meet with it face to face. It is likely too, apart from the influence of her husband, that it was early memories of Kennington that drew her as a young woman into The Fabian Society.

What was that house like of which E. Nesbit became so fond that houses were to haunt all her children's books? It would have been comfortable, and certainly up-to-date, for the agricultural college had been modernised ten years before she arrived. It was the William Morris period, and the Nesbits were a go-ahead family, so the walls could have been covered with Morris wallpapers, and the house could have been full of his furniture. But the college had been founded by John Nesbit's father, so it is more likely it was inherited furniture and inherited wallpapers with which the Nesbit children grew up, for at the time of E. Nesbit's birth the income tax was 1s. 4d. in the pound, which was considered dangerously high, so, comfortably off though the Nesbits were, it was unlikely they had remoulded their home to fit in with William Morris's ideas. So it can be supposed that the room in which the child first opened her eyes was a Victorian bedroom of no particular date. The lighting of the bedroom and throughout the house would be by lamps and candles, for gas lighting, though E. Nesbit saw it as a child, was not generally used until much later in the century. Not that gas or even electricity being common-place at the time at which she was writing, would have troubled her, for throughout her children's books she used what suited her, so if she fancied reverting to candles she reverted to them without explanation.

E. Nesbit had a gift, shared by other great children's writers, for recapturing the timelessness of childhood, the vast tracts of time that lie between one Christmas and the next, from birthday to birthday, and though the gift of memory was born in her, she was helped in that she arrived in the world at a pleasantly slow moving period. She belonged to the days when a nursery was a "must" in all well-to-do homes. The majority of E. Nesbit's readers today, whose play-room is the living-room floor, can have no idea what a nursery was. When she was a child it was not necessarily a nice room, for at that period when children were supposed to be seen and not heard, and discipline was strong and any form of pampering believed to be harmful, the charming nurseries of a later day would not have been thought of. But it was the children's own room, and it was ruled by a nurse, probably assisted by an under-nurse, and though adults came into it, they were visitors, and when they left the nursery would with its rocking horse, dolls' house, and high fire guard, slip back into its normal slow tempo. Describing her own childhood there is nothing about nurseries though she writes affectionately about her nurse, but in her books the world of nurseries is implied by the feeling of unlimited leisure being a child's right. Always her families belong to the days when children were supposed to be children, shut off from grown-up cares, and grown-up chores. Nobody in a Nesbit book says 'Whose turn is it to do the washing-up?'

There were five surviving Nesbit children, the eldest Saretta, was a daughter by Sarah Nesbit's first marriage. Then came Mary, a very delicate girl, then two brothers, Alfred and Henry, and finally Edith. As will be shown, somewhat naturally because they were nearest to her in age, there was an immense bond of affection between E. Nesbit and her brothers. This book, as already explained, is not intended to be a life of E. Nesbit, but an attempt only to understand her magic, and from what it sprang. But it seems necessary to give a brief outline of her history, so we skip to the year 1880. She was then not quite twenty-one, and at a registrar's office in London she married young Hubert Bland. From the date of that marriage until fame came to her, she lived an incredibly hard life. She bore eight children, of which three died in infancy, and one, Fabian, when he was fourteen, as well, she felt it incumbent on her to adopt two more. Yet at no time was she really fond of children and until her children were almost grown up she was deadly poor, in what for a less resilient character would have been a soul-destroying making-two-ends-meet way.

What had happened was that Hubert Bland, who had a small business when she married him, was almost at once taken desperately ill with small-pox, and while he was struggling back to life his partner in his little business ran off abroad with their whole capital. This meant the young Blands were practically penniless, and the wolf was only kept from the door by E. Nesbit's earnings as a writer for women's papers, and newspapers, and as a reciter at small functions such as smoking concerts.

From all accounts and from her photographs, E. Nesbit was an exceptionally good-looking young woman, but not when young robust in appearance, so she seemed unfitted for a life of drudgery. Yet she squared her shoulders, kept up her chin, remained young in heart, and somehow kept the home going. This period of her life, as will be shown, resulted in one of her best, if not the best, of her children's books. After Hubert Bland recovered from his long illness he became a journalist, not a very successful one, for the family was to remain hard-up until E. Nesbit wrote seriously for children, which she did not do until she was almost forty. But lack of money was not allowed to fetter them, for it was in these years that

E. NESBIT AGED THREE

E. NESBIT WITH HER NURSE – 1864

the Blands became the couple they wished the world to recognize. She the fascinating, though temperamental woman, he monocled and top-hatted, what was known in those days as a dandy, both very considerable figures in The Fellowship of New Life, which later became The Fabian Society, of which they were founder members.

When money began to come E. Nesbit's way she bought the house which was to be her home until 1921. It was called Well Hall, and was at Eltham. This house was for many years an unofficial meeting place for Fabians; it was a big rambling barrack of a house, with the doors always open to friends and acquaintances, and a meal of sorts for all who cared to eat it. About this time there were summer holidays at Dymchurch in the house which is now Dymchurch Vicarage, where the same sort of hospitality went on as at Well Hall. To Dymchurch, and the surrounding neighbourhood, came friends and devotees, for the Blands were the centre of an interesting bohemian group.

It is hard to judge how deeply the Blands felt about The Fabian Society, for accounts are conflicting. H. G. Wells in his *Experiment in Autobiography* states he thought Hubert Bland a poseur, and found both the Blands 'fundamentally intricate'. To him they were trouble-makers for the fun of the thing, the sort of people who could not see anything working happily and smoothly without an overwhelming compulsion to snarl it up. Writing of The Fabian Society meetings he says that when the Blands were present 'anonymous letters flittered about like bats at twilight'. That there are such people as Wells believed the Blands to be is, of course, a fact, there can be few who have not suffered from them, but Wells'

B

assessment of them may easily have been wrong. He came from a simple, straight-forward home, and would have found even mild sophistry puzzling. Moreover, he was a young ardent Fabian enthusiast, and was no doubt impatient to see the beginnings of that new world that was planned, and when there were delays looked for people on whom to pin the blame.

In 1910 Hubert Bland's health broke. He had suffered from heart trouble for some years, but now his eyesight began to go until he was totally blind. He died in 1914 just before the outbreak of World War One. The four years of his illness had been hard ones for E. Nesbit, for not only was her husband able to earn nothing, but her own earnings began to drop. She still kept Well Hall going, but with little of its former glory. In Doris Langley Moore's *E. Nesbit, a Biography* there are letters written at this time which show how hard her life was. 'I wish,' she wrote to her brother Harry, 'everyone had a small pension to live on at 50 – enough to live on.' And well she might make such a wish, for Hubert's illness was costing a lot of money, and the strain of looking after him, and being his eyes, while struggling to write her own books, must have bowed even her gay spirit.

E. Nesbit spent the war years living in Well Hall. She still kept open house, and as well took paying guests, though how she managed puzzled everybody, for the servants had left to go into war work, food was scarce, and she herself writing all day. But it must have been clear to her that she could not much longer manage her home alone, and then in 1917 she married again. Her second husband was an old friend, a Mr. Tucker, known to everybody as 'The Skipper'. This marriage, which made her last years

very happy, is the end of the E. Nesbit history. She
and The Skipper lived on for a short time at Well
Hall, and then he took her to a sort of bungalow at a
place that was then called Jesson St. Mary on Rom-
ney Marsh, but is now St. Mary's Bay. Not that E.
Nesbit retired into obscurity, she never did that, to
the end of her life admirers of her books for children
made pilgrimages to visit her. One such pilgrim was
Noël Coward. He writes:

'Her books have meant a very great deal to me,
not only while I was a little boy of nine and onwards,
but right up to the present day. I have re-read them
each at least twenty times.

'It was in 1922 that I first met her, she was living
near Dymchurch and I went boldly and called on her.
I found her absolutely charming, with greyish-white
hair and a rather sharp sense of humour. Her husband, "The Skipper", and she were living in a sort
of Nissen hut at Jesson St. Mary's, between Dymchurch and Littlestone.

'I told her how much I admired her books and we
became friends. After this first visit I saw her on and
off until she died.

'My favourites of her books are, in the following
order, *Five Children and It*, *The Phoenix and the Carpet*, *The House of Arden*, *The Enchanted Castle*, *The
Wonderful Garden*, and the Bastable books.

'I can't, after all these years, remember her very
clearly, but, as I say, her books I never forget. She
had an economy of phrase, and an unparalleled talent
for evoking hot summer days in the English countryside.'

E. Nesbit died in Jesson St. Mary on a bed which

was specially raised so that she could look out on what she described in her last poem as 'The little lovely hills of Kent'. She was buried in the churchyard of St. Mary's the Marsh, and her grave is marked by a wooden memorial carved for her by The Skipper. It is two wooden uprights with a crossbar on which is written: 'Resting. E. Nesbit. Mrs. Bland-Tucker. Poet and Author died 4th May 1924 aged 65.'

If E. Nesbit could see that bungalow in which she died now, she would be pleased to find the view quite unchanged, except that the miniature railway runs past the bottom of her garden, and at the end of tiny Nesbit Road, as it is now called, is the miniature railway station of St. Mary's Bay. For always homes had meant so much to her, and though she did not live to write about her last one, it would have joined with Well Hall, the house in Lewisham, the rented homes of her childhood, and the Agricultural College in Kennington Lane, to emerge from the storeroom of her memory as 'our ancestral home in the Lewisham Road'. 'The jolly big red house on Blackheath.' 'A little red-roofed house.' 'The bright-faced house with bow windows.' 'Three Chimneys.' 'The Moat House', and 'The White House'. Each with its own personality, and each so vividly described.

❖❖❖❖❖❖❖❖❖❖❖❖❖❖❖❖❖❖❖❖❖❖❖❖❖❖❖❖❖❖

CHAPTER TWO

School Days

❖❖❖❖❖❖❖❖❖❖❖❖❖❖❖❖❖❖❖❖❖❖❖❖❖❖❖❖❖❖

E. NESBIT wrote of her own childhood that she was able to write about it 'not because my childhood was different from that of others, not because I have anything strange to relate, anything new to tell, are these words written. For the other reason rather – that I was a child as other children, that my memories are their memories, as my hopes were their hopes, my dreams their dreams, my fears their fears – I open the book of memory to tear out some pages for you others.

'There is nothing here that is not in my most clear and vivid recollection.

'When I was a little child I used to pray fervently, tearfully, that when I should be grown up I might never forget what I thought and felt and suffered then.

'Let these pages speak for me, and bear witness that I have not forgotten.'

It is curious that E. Nesbit should have written these words, for her childhood was different from that of others, and it is interesting that she never realised how unusual it was. Her father died before she was five, and soon after that her home was broken up, and much of her childhood was spent abroad, but even while her father was alive she does not seem to have led the conventional life of a child of her date and class. For one thing there was apparently little or no church going, most unusual at a time when it was customary to attend some place of worship from respectability if not from devotion. So little do her family seem to have cared what the neighbours thought that they did not have the child christened until she could walk to the font, and, however unintelligibly, make her own vows, which must have caused eyebrows to be raised and tongues to have clacked. Then the children do not seem to have been kept to their nursery, as their contemporaries would have been. Nesbit herself refers to a nurse and an under-nurse, but they cannot have been the dominant personalities we, who were brought up by nurses, remember, or surely a nannie whose slightest word was a law which could not be broken would have crept into one of her books. Nor, judging by the lives of the children in her stories, would it seem as if the generally accepted 'coming down after tea' played any part. If her nurse had changed every garment she wore, put her hair into ringlets, and buttoned her into a party frock every tea-time to go down to the drawing-room the same fate must surely have befallen some of her fiction children. But no, the whole lot live a gloriously free life, which no doubt caused much envy in the hearts of the young Edwardians who first read about them.

Then the child herself was unusual. A passionate little creature, very emotional, but full of affection, and vividly aware of the joy of being alive, but equally she suffered deeply. When she prayed so fervently that she might never forget what she had thought and felt and suffered her prayer was answered, for it is because the children she created think and feel and suffer that they live. It is easy to imagine the little Nesbit who, from her photograph was the most attractive child, living intensely every minute of those early years in Kennington, and as she lived recording, for she was one of the fortunate who was born with a blotting-paper memory. She never forgot what it had felt like to be a child, the excitement and smell of a new day, the crushing fears which she herself described most vividly, and the equally inexplicable ecstasies. She knew then, and she never lost the knowledge, the unclimbable barrier that lies between a child and a grown-up – even the best of grown-ups. She knew too the avalanches of grief that were so solid they could suffocate, especially when it appeared the grief was due to an injustice. She knew what it was like to be intolerably bored, and to have to accept the boredom. Then there was her nose, her books are full of the smells of childhood: bonfires and new-mown grass, and the joy of lying flat on the ground to listen to small unnameable noises. Yet, thinking back on her childhood, it is not these qualities she writes about, but her fears.

'How can I write of it, sitting here in the shifting shade of the lime-trees, with the sunny daisied grass stretching away my ears filled with the soft swish-swish of the gardener's scythe at the other end of the lawn, and the merry little voices of the children away in the meadow?

'Only by shutting my eyes and ears to the sweet sounds and sights of summer and the sun can I recall at all for you the dead silences, the frozen terrors of the long, dark nights when I was little, and lonely, and very very much afraid.

'The first thing I remember that frightened me was running into my father's dressing-room and finding him playing at wild beasts with my brothers. He wore his great fur travelling coat inside out, and his roars were completely convincing. I was borne away screaming, and dreamed of wild beasts for many a long night afterwards.

'Then came some nursery charades. I was the high-born orphan, whom gipsies were to steal, and my part was to lie in a cradle, and, at the proper moment, to be carried away shrieking. I understood my part perfectly – I was about three, I suppose – and had rehearsed it more than once. Being carried off in the arms of the gipsy (my favourite sister) was nothing to scream at, I thought, but she told me to scream, and I did it. Unfortunately, however, there had beeen no dress rehearsals, and when, on the night of the performance the high-born orphan found itself close to a big black bonnet and a hideous mask, it did scream to some purpose, and presently screamed itself into some some sort of fit or swoon, was put to bed, and stayed there for many days which passed dream-like. But that old woman haunted my dreams for years – haunts them still indeed. I tell you I come across her in my dreams to this day. She bends over me and puts her face close to mine, and I wake with a spasm of agonised terror; only now it is not horrible to me to waken "in the dark". I draw a few long breaths and as soon as my heart beats a little less wildly I fall asleep again. But a child who wakes from an ugly dream does not fall asleep so quickly. For to a child who is frightened, the darkness and the silence of its lonely room are only a shade less terrible than the wild horrors of dreamland. One used to lie awake in the silence, listening, listening to the pad-pad of one's heart, straining one's ears to make sure that it was not the pad-pad of something else, something un-speakable creeping towards one out of the horrible dense dark. One used to lie quite, quite still, I remember, listening, listening. And when my nurse came to bed and tucked me up, she used to find my pillow wet, and say to the under-nurse:

'"Weakness, you know. The precious poppet doesn't seem to get any stronger.'

'But my pillow was not wet with tears of weakness. These were the dews of agony and terror.

'My nurse – ah, how good she was to me – never went downstairs to supper after she found out my terrors, which she very quickly did. She used to sit in the day nursery with the door open "a tiny crack", and that light was company, because I knew I had only to call out, and someone who loved me would come and banish fear. But a light without human companionship was worse than darkness, especially a little light. Night-lights, deepening the shadows with their horrid possibilities are a mere refinement of cruelty, and some friends who thought to do me a kindness by leaving the gas burning low gave me one of the most awful nights I ever had.

'It was a strange house in Sutherland Gardens – a house with large rooms and heavy hangings – with massive wardrobes and deep ottoman boxes. The immense four-post beds stood out about a yard from the wall, for some "convenience of sweeping" reason, I believe. Consider the horror of having behind you, as you lay trembling in the chill linen of a strange bed, a dark space, from which, even now, in the black silence something might be stealthily creeping – something which would presently lean over you, in the dark – whose touch you would feel, not knowing whether it were the old woman in the mask or some new terror.

'That was the torture of the first night. The next I

begged that the gas might be left "full on". It was, and I fell asleep in comparative security. But while I slept, came some thrifty soul, and finding the gas "burning to waste" turned it down. Not out – down.

'I awoke in a faint light, and presently sat up in bed to see where it came from, and this is what I saw. A corpse laid out under white draperies, and at its foot a skeleton with luminous skull and outstretched bony arm.

'I knew, somewhere far away and deep down, my reason knew that the dead body was a white dress laid on a long ottoman, that the skull was the opal globe of the gas and the arm the pipe of the gas-bracket, but that was not reason's hour. Imagination held sway, and her poor little victim, who was ten years old then, and ought to have known better, sat up in bed, hour after hour, with the shadowy void behind her. The dark curtains on each side, and in front that horror.

'Next day I went home, which was perhaps a good thing for my brain.

'When my father was alive we lived in a big house in Kennington Lane, where he taught young men agriculture and chemistry. My father had a big mea-dow and garden, and had a sort of small farm there. Fancy a farm at Kennington!

'Among the increase that blessed his shed was a two-headed calf. The head and shoulders of this were stuffed, and inspired me with a terror which my brothers increased by pursuing me with the terrible object. But one of my father's pupils to whom I owe that and many other kindnesses, one day seized me under one arm and the two-headed horror under the other, and thus equipped we pursued my brothers. They fled shrieking, and I never feared it again.

'In a dank, stone-flagged room where the boots were blacked, and the more unwieldly chemicals housed, there was nailed on the wall the black skin of an emu. That skin, with its wiry black feathers that fluttered dismally in the draught, was no mere bird's skin to me. It hated me, it wished me ill. It was always lurking for me in the dark, ready to rush out at me. It was waiting for me at the top of the flight, while the old woman with the mask stretched skinny hands out to grasp my little legs as I went up the nursery stairs. I never passed the skin without covering my eyes with my hands. From this terror that walked by night I was delivered by a Mr. Kearns, now public analyst for Sheffield. He took me on his shoulder, where I felt quite safe, reluctant but not resisting, to within a couple of yards of the emu.

'"Now," he said, "will you do what I tell you?"

'"Not any nearer," I said evasively.

'"Now you know I won't let it hurt you."

'"Yes."

'"Then will you stroke it, if I do first?"

'I didn't want to.

'"To please me."

'That argument was conclusive, for I loved him.

'Then we approached the black feathers, I clinging desperately to his neck, and sobbing convulsively.

'"No – no – no – not any nearer!"

'But he was kind and wise, and insisted. His big hand smoothed down the feathers.

'"Now, Daisy. You know you promised. Give me your hand."

'I shut my eyes tight, and let him draw my hand down the dusty feathers. Then I opened my eyes a little bit.

'"Now you stroke it. Stroke the poor emu."

'I did so.

'"Are you afraid now?"'

'Curiously enough I wasn't. Poor Mr. Kearns paid dearly for his kindness. For several weeks I gave him no peace, but insisted on being taken, at all hours of the day and night to "stroke the poor emu". So proud is one of a new courage.

'After we left Kennington, I seem to have had a period of more ordinary terrors – of dreams from which to awaken was mere relief; not a horror scarcely less than that of the dream itself. I dreamed of cows and dogs, of falling houses, and crumbling precipices.'

In writing of her fears, Nesbit has probably pointed to one reason why she had such a gift for writing for children. Temperamental, wilful, and fiery-tempered though the child was, she was on the surface surrounded by most of the things that a child needs. It is true that she lost her father before she was five, and her home not long after, but she had her mother whom she adored, yet in her own description of her fears she shows that basically she was unhappy, and without doubt an unhappy childhood is the best possible training for those who are going to write for children. The happy child looking back on childhood seems to see everything in a pink glow: summers are always hot, in winter there is always snow, Christmases and birthdays were always perfect. If there were disappointments, Christmas spent in bed with influenza, a birthday in the dark because of measles, it is all swamped in the memory of a radiant, glorious childhood. To Nesbit her childhood was never radiant, probably from the earliest age, otherwise she would not have stood back from it looking at it, and thinking to herself: 'When I have children this won't happen to them'. Carefully she stored her impressions away in her author's lumber room of a mind, and there they lay until she was forty. She only had to open the door of her mind and out came her childhood, fresh as the day she had put it away. And she remained true to the child she had once been, determining that things were not going to be like that for her children, though of course in a different way they were, for each child had his or her own personality and tastes, and what their mother had wanted so desperately when she was a child was not always what they wanted. But for the children in her books it was different, for them there was to be a glorious carefree childhood, where nothing was too wonderful to happen. And so, using her memory and all her senses, she drew from her mind her children's books. But she was far too much of an artist to believe that children liked everything to be easy; she remembered there must be some obstacles over which to triumph, and so she was always inventing them. *The Wouldbegoods* opens with the sentence 'Children are like jam: all very well in the proper place, but you can't stand them all over the shop – eh, what?' To which remark Oswald commented: 'Your lot is indeed a dark and a terrible one when your father is ashamed of you. And we all knew this, so that we felt in our chests just as if we had swallowed a hard-boiled egg whole.'

What a terrible feeling that was of having swallowed a hard-boiled egg whole, and who cannot remember it, how it seemed to grow, of the terror it brought when the hard-boiled egg feeling occurred in an unsuitable place, so that at any minute there might be the final shame of tears.

Little Nesbit, though she suffered from her own temperament, and indeed suffered from it all her life, only knew imaginary fears when she lived in Kennington. Real suffering and loneliness she was not to know until later. All lovers of Nesbit's books must therefore be grateful to Kennington Lane, the house, the garden, the field and the little farm, for there, as a small thing, the child learned to love a house. She learnt other things besides of course, but loving a house came high upon the list, and was the first step towards that far distant day when she would take up her pen and write Chapter One, *The Story of the Treasure Seekers*.

CHAPTER THREE

Brighton and
Buckinghamshire

JOHN NESBIT died in 1862, and Sarah Nesbit, who
had already been widowed once, might well have
taken to her sofa and smelling bottle, for it was a
period when both were much in use, and well thought
of. Instead, for a time, she ran the agricultural college, a remarkable effort for a woman who, as far as is
known, had no qualifications for the task. But Mary's
health was giving anxiety, as it did until her death
before she was twenty, so when Edith was seven we
find the family established temporarily in Brighton.
Presumably there was less money after John Nesbit's
death, for by the time the family reached Brighton
there appear to have been no nurses, and as the Nesbits never, as far as can be discovered, went in for
governesses, and as presumably Mrs. Nesbit had
enough on her hands running the house and looking
after Mary, the small Edith was sent to a boarding
school.

It is likely, though the child was too small to feel
her father's death acutely, she had been upset by the
event, and still more by the feeling of impending
change, for naturally plans must have been constantly
discussed. Certainly the child who emerges from
Nesbit's own description of that Brighton school is a

changed small girl from the one whose fears she wrote about. For that child, who had been able to communicate her fear of the emu to Mr. Kearns, of the two-headed calf to her father's pupil, and of the dark to her nurse, is gone, for what she suffered at Brighton she kept to herself. E. Nesbit's daughter, Mrs. Philips, says that all her life through her mother refused to endure small troubles, but would suffer big ones with fortitude. Did the small rather spoilt, highly-strung, temperamental child find the little fiend in the Brighton school whom she faced alone at the age of seven a big trouble? Here is her description of what happened:

'The first school I went to was a Mrs. Arthur's – at Brighton. I remember very little about the lessons, because I was only seven years old, but I remember – to my inmost fibre I remember the play. There was a yard behind the house – no garden, and there I used to play with another small child whose name I have forgotten. But I know that she wore a Stuart plaid frock, and that I detested her.

'On the first day of my arrival we were sent into the "playground" with our toys. Stuart plaid, as I must call her, having no other name, had a battered doll and three scallop-shells. I had a very complete little set of pewter tea-things in a cardboard box.

'"Let's change for a bit," said Stuart plaid.

'Mingled politeness and shyness compelled my acquiescence. She took my new tea-things, and I disconsolately nursed the battered torso of her doll. But this grew very wearisome, and I, feeling satisfied that the claims of courtesy had been fully met, protested mildly.

'"Now then," said Stuart plaid, looking up from

SARAH NESBIT — E. NESBIT'S MOTHER

WELL HALL – THE NESBITS' HOUSE

the tea-things, "don't be so selfish; besides, they're horrid little stupid tin things. I wouldn't give twopence for them."

'"But I don't want you to give twopence for them; I want them back."

'"Oh, no you don't!"

'"Yes I do," said I, roused by her depreciation of my property, "and I'll have them too, so there!"

'I advanced towards her – I am afraid with some half-formed determination of pulling her hair.

'"All right," she said, "you stand there and I'll put them in the box and give them to you."

'"Promise!"

'"Yes, if you don't move."

'She turned her back on me. It took her a very long time to put them in the box. I stood tingling with indignation, and a growing desire to slap her face. Presently she turned.

'"You would have them back," she said, grinning unpleasantly, "and here they are."

'She put them into my hands. She had bitten every single cup, saucer, and plate into a formless lump!

'While I stood speechless with anger and misery, she came close to me and said tauntingly –

'"There, now! Aren't you sorry you didn't let me have them?'

'"I'll go home," I said, struggling between pride and tears.

'"Oh, no you won't," said Stuart plaid, thrusting her mocking face close to mine; "and if you say a word about it I'll say you did it and pinched me as well. And Mrs. Arthur'll believe me, because I'm not a new girl, and you are!"

'I turned away without a word, and I never did

c

tell – till now. But I never said another word to
Stuart plaid out of school. She tortured me unremit-
tingly. When I had been at school a week or two my
paint-box suffered at her hands, but I bore meekly in
silence, only seeking to replace my Vandyke brown
by mud from the garden. Chinese white I sought to
manufacture by a mixture of chalk picked up on the
sea-shore, and milk from my mug at tea-time. It was
never a successful industry. I remember the hot white
streets, and the flies, and Brill's baths, and the West-
ern Road, and the bitter pang of passing, at the end
of a long procession, our own house, where always
someone might be at the window, and never anyone
was. I used to go home on Saturdays, and then all
bitterness was so swallowed up in the bliss of the
home-returning, that I actually forgot the miseries of
my school-life; but I was very unhappy there. Mrs.
Arthur and the big girls were kind enough to me, but
Stuart plaid was enough to blight any lot. She
blighted mine, and I suppose no prisoner ever hailed
the falling of his fetters with the joy I felt when at
last, after three or four days of headache and tears, I
was wrapped in a blanket and taken home with the
measles.

'When I got better we went for the mid-summer
holidays to a lovely cottage among the beech-woods
of Buckinghamshire. I shall never forget the sense of
rest and delight that filled my small heart when I
slipped out under the rustic porch at five o'clock the
first morning, and felt the cool velvet turf under my
feet. Brighton pavement had been so hard and hot.
Then, instead of the long rows of dazzling houses
with their bow windows and green-painted balconies,
there were lovely trees, acacias and elms, and a big
copper beech. In the school walks we never had found

any flowers but little pink bind-weed, by the dusty roadside. Here there were royal red roses, and jasmine, and tall white lilies, and in the hedge by the gate, sweet-briar and deep-cupped white convolvulus. I think I saw then for the first time how lovely God's good world is, and ever since then, thank God, I have been seeing it more and more. That was a happy morning.

'The boys – whom I had not seen for ever so long, because of the measles – were up already. Alfred had a rabbit for me – a white rabbit with pink eyes – in a hutch he had made himself. And Harry led me to a nook among the roots of the copper beech, where he showed me two dormice in an old tea-caddy.

'"You shall go shares in them if you like," he said.

'There was honey in the comb for breakfast, and new-laid eggs, and my mother was there in a cool cotton gown pouring out tea, and purring with pleasure at having all her kittens together again. There were cool raspberries on the table too, trimmed with fresh green leaves, and through the window we saw the fruit garden and its promise. That was summer indeed.

'After breakfast my mother called me to her – she had some patterns in her hand.

'"You must be measured for some new frocks, Daisy," she said.

'"Oh, how nice. What colour?"

'"Well, some nice white ones, and this pretty plaid."

'She held up a pattern as she spoke. It was a Stuart plaid.

'"Oh, not that!" I cried.

'"Not this pretty plaid, darling? Why not?"

'If you'll believe me, I could not say why not. And the frock was made, and I wore it, loathing it, till the

day when I fell out of the apple-tree, and it broke my
fall by catching on a branch. But it saved my life at
the expense of its own; and I gave a feast to all the
dolls to celebrate its interment in the rag-bag.

'I have often wondered what it is that keeps children from telling their mothers these things – and
even now I don't know. I only know I might have
been saved many of these little-big troubles if I had
only been able to explain. But I wasn't; and to this
day my mother does not know how and why I hated
that Stuart plaid frock.'

The rapture of being carried home with the measles,
and the warmth with which she describes the cottage
in Buckinghamshire, are the Nesbit of the children's
books, but nowhere in her stories can I find the Nesbit
who knew what it was like to have to put up with a
little horror such as Stuart plaid. In fact her books
are curiously free from nasty children; Albert-next-
door is no worse than The Indian Uncle's description
of him as 'a muff', and Daisy and Denny, who appeared unlikely material at the beginning of *The
Wouldbegoods*, by the finish of the book were as much
a part of the family as H. O. himself.

E. Nesbit was not an all-children-are-darlings
author, and even in her most magical moments believed that more than beautiful thoughts were needed,
if her characters were to float into the air. Why then
did she never write about a really horrible child?
She had first-hand knowledge of such a one, so vividly
remembered, that she could write about her in middle
life as if she had seen her yesterday. The answer
lies in the reason already given. In her children's
books E. Nesbit drew childhood as she thought it
ought to be, and as indeed it is for many children,

carefree, every day a new adventure. All her children
have faults, but ordinary every-day family sins only,
for hers is an idyllic children's world, where little
horrors like Stuart plaid, though she knew they existed, could never find a place, for her fiction children
had no idea that such unpleasant types were in the
world. Her children in all her books are fundamentally as 'The Poor Indian', afterwards 'Our Indian
Uncle', described them 'The jolliest little cubs I
ever saw!'

Of course, like all children of temperament, at the
top of the rainbow one minute, face downwards on
the ground the next, the child knew periods of passionate happiness, and because so much of her childhood was grim, was conscious in every fibre of being
happy when she was happy. It is likely she even put
it into words: 'This is my lovely day. This is me being
happy,' and these periods she cherished in her heart
and gave to her children readers. Had she not had
this ability to appreciate childish happiness when she
had it, it is doubtful if she could have written her
books, for much of the childhood she remembered
and wrote about could have a place in a book by
Dickens. Mrs. Nesbit appears to have had no gift
when picking schools. This description by E. Nesbit
herself of the school she next went to at Stamford, to
which she must have been sent when she was still
small, for it was a mixed school, which of course
schools of the period for older girls were not, is really
heart-breaking.

'I spent a year in the select boarding establish-
ment for young ladies and gentlemen at Stamford,
and I venture to think that I should have preferred a
penal settlement. Miss Fairfield whose school it was,
was tall and pale and dark, and I thought her as good

and beautiful as an angel. I don't know now whether she was really beautiful, but I know she was good. And her mother – dear soul – had a sympathy with small folk in disgrace, which has written her name in gold letters on my heart.

'But there was another person in the house, whose name I will not put down. She came continually between me and my adored Miss Fairfield. She had a sort of influence over me which made it impossible for me ever to do anything well while she was near me. Miss Fairfield's health compelled her to leave much to Miss — , and I was, in consequence, as gloomy a cynic as any child of my age in Lincoln-shire. My chief troubles were three – my hair, my hands, and my arithmetic.

'My hair was never tidy – I don't know why. Per-haps it runs in the family – for my little daughter's head is just as rough as mine used to be. This got me into continual disgrace. I am sure I tried hard enough to keep it tidy – I brushed it for fruitless hours till my little head was so sore that it hurt me to put my hat on. But it never would look smooth and shiny, like Katie Martin's, nor would it curl prettily like the red locks of Cissy Thomas. It was always a rough, impossible brown mop. I got into a terrible scrape for trying to soften it by an invention of my own. As we all know, Burleigh House is by Stamford Town, and in Burleigh Park we children took our daily constitutional. We played under the big oaks there, and were bored to extinction, not because we dis-liked the park, but because we went there every day at the same hour.

'Now Harry Martin (he wore striped stockings and was always losing his handkerchief) suffered from his hair almost as much as I did; so when I unfolded my plan to him one day in the park, he joyfully agreed to help me.

'We each gathered a pocketful of acorns, and when we went to wash our hands before dinner, we cut up some of the acorns into little bits, and put them into the doll's bath with some cold water and a little scent that Cissy Thomas gave us, out of a bottle she had bought for twopence at the fair at home.

'"This," I said, "will be acorn oil – scented acorn oil."

'"Will it?" said Harry doubtfully.

'"Yes," I replied, adding confidentially, "and there is nothing better for the hair."

'But we never had a chance of even seeing whether acorns and water would turn to oil – a miracle which I entirely believed in. The dinner bell rang, and I only had time hastily to conceal the doll's bath at the back of the cupboard where Miss —— kept her dresses. That was Saturday.

'Next day we found that Miss ——'s best dress (the blue silk with the Bismark brown gimp) had slipped from its peg and fallen on to the doll's bath. The dress was ruined, and when Harry Martin and I owned up, as in honour bound – Miss Fairfield was away in London – we were deprived of dinner, and had a long Psalm to learn. I don't know whether punishment affects the hair, but I thought, next morning at prayers, that Harry's tow-crop looked more like hay than ever.

'My hands were more compromising to me than anyone would have believed who had ever seen their size, for, in the winter especially, they were never clean. I can see now the little willow-patterned basin of hard cold water, and smell the unpleasant little square of mottled soap with which I was expected to wash them. I don't know how the others managed, but for me the result was always the same – failure; and when I presented myself at breakfast, trying to hide my red and grubby paws in my pinafore, Miss — used to say:

'"Show your hands, Daisy – yes, as I thought. Not fit to sit down with young ladies and gentlemen. Breakfast in the schoolroom for Miss Daisy."

'Then little Miss Daisy would shiveringly betake herself to the cold, bare schoolroom, where the fire had but just been kindled.

'I used to sit cowering over the damp sticks with my white mug – mauve spotted it was I remember, and had a brown crack near the handle – on a chair beside me. Sometimes I used to pull a twig from the fire, harpoon my bread-and-butter with it, and hold it to the fire: the warm, pale, greasy result I called toast.

'All this happened when Miss Fairfield was laid up with bronchitis. It was at that time, too, that my battle with compound long division began. Now I was not, I think, a very dull child, and always had an indignant sense that I could do sums well enough if anyone would tell me what they meant. But no one did, and day after day the long division sums, hopelessly wrong, disfigured my slate, and were washed off with my tears. Day after day I was sent to bed, my dinner was knocked off, or my breakfast, or my tea. I should literally have starved, I do believe, but for dear Mrs. Fairfield. She kept my little body going with illicit cakes and plums and the like, and fed my starving little heart with surreptitious kisses and kind words. She would lie in wait for me as I passed down the hall, and in a whisper call me into the store closet. It had a mingled and delicious smell of pickles and tea and oranges and jam, and the one taper Mrs. Fairfield carried only lighted dimly the delightful mystery of its well-filled shelves. Mrs. Fairfield used to give me a great lump of cake or a broad slice of bread and jam, and lock me into the dark cupboard till it was eaten. I never taste black-currant jam now without a strong memory of the dark hole of happiness, where I used to wait – my sticky fingers held well away from my pinafore – till Mrs. Fairfield's heavy step and jingling keys came to release me. Then she would sponge my hands and face and send me away clean, replete, and with a better heart for the eternal conflict with long division.

'I fancy that when Miss Fairfield came downstairs again she changed the field of my arithmetical studies; for during the spring I seem to remember a blessed respite from my troubles. It is true that Miss — was away, staying with friends.

'I was very popular at school that term I remember, for I had learned to make doll's bedsteads out of match-boxes during the holidays, and my eldest sister's Christmas present provided me with magnificent hangings for the same. Imagine a vivid green silk sash, with brilliant butterflies embroidered all over it in coloured silk and gold thread. A long sash, too, from which one could well spare a few inches at a time for upholstery. I acquired many marbles, and much ginger-bread, and totally eclipsed Cissy Thomas who had enjoyed the fleeting sunshine of popular favour on the insecure basis of paper dolls. Over my memory of this term no long division cast its hateful shade, and the scolding my dear mother gave me when she saw my sash's fair proportions docked to a waistband and a hard knot, with two brief and irregular ends, was so gentle that I endured it with fortitude, and considered my ten weeks of popularity cheaply bought. I went back to school in high spirits with a new set of sashes and some magnificent pieces of silk and lace from my mother's lavendered wardrobe.

'But no one wanted dolls' beds any more; and Cissy Thomas had brought back a herbarium: the others all became botanists, and I, after a faint effort to emulate their successes, fell back on my garden.

'The seeds I had set in the spring had had a rest during the Easter holidays, and were already sprouting greenly, but alas, I never saw them flower. Long division set in again. Again, day after day, I sat lonely in the schoolroom – now like a furnace – and ate my dry bread and milk and water in the depths of disgrace, with the *faux commencements* and those revolting sums staring at me from my tear-blotted slate.

'Night after night I cried myself to sleep in my bed – whose coarse home-spun sheets were hotter than blankets – because I could not get the answers right. Even Miss Fairfield, I fancied, began to look coldly on me, and the other children naturally did not care to associate with one so deficient in arithmetic.

'One evening as I was sitting as usual sucking the smooth, dark slate pencil, and grieving over my troubles with the heart-broken misery of a child, to whom the present grief looks eternal, I heard a carriage drive up to the door. Our schoolroom was at the back, and I was too much interested in a visitor – especially one who came at that hour and in a carriage – to be able to bear the suspense of that silent schoolroom, so I cautiously opened its door and crept on hands and knees across the passage and

looked down through the banisters. They were opening the door. It was a lady, and Mrs. Fairfield came
out of the dining-room to meet her. It was a lady in a
black moiré antique dress and Paisley shawl of the
then mode. It was a lady whose face I could not see,
because her back was to the red sunset light; but at
that moment she spoke and the next I was clinging
round the moiré skirts with my head buried in the
Paisley shawl. The world, all upside down, had suddenly righted itself. I, who had faced it alone, now
looked out at it from the secure shelter of a moiré
screen – for my mother had come to see me.

'I did not cry myself to sleep that night, because
my head lay on her arm. But even then I could not
express how wretched I had been. Only when I heard
that my mother was going to the South of France
with my sisters, I clung about her neck, and with such
insistence implored her not to leave me – not to go
without me, that I think I must have expressed my
trouble without uttering it, for when, after three
delicious days of drives and walks, in which I had
always a loving hand to hold, my mother left Stamford, she took me – trembling with joy like a prisoner
reprieved – with her.'

In that last paragraph almost certainly lies a large
part of the Nesbit magic.

Fears

DELIGHTED BY the prospect of never having to
return to the school at Stamford, the child set off
happily on her journey to France, too small to realise
apparently that there would no longer be a place in
England that she could call home. The journey to
France had been planned by Sarah Nesbit on two
counts: first Mary's health, but as well there was
Saretta to consider. Being the daughter by Sarah
Nesbit's first marriage the girl was older than her
half-sisters and brothers, and naturally did not want
to be tied down to a house full of children still at school;
the answer to Mrs. Nesbit seemed to be foreign travel,
which would be a real killing of two birds with one
stone, for Mary's health might benefit, and surely
Saretta would find gay friends in France.

It was clearly not Sarah Nesbit's intention originally that Edith should be part of the party, for travelling with a young child was at that date a nuisance,
for although it was becoming accepted that passen-
gers should have some means of communication with
the guard and the conductor, there were no corridors
on trains, which meant clambering out at stations to
go to the lavatory, and carrying your food with you in
picnic baskets. Lighting at that time in English trains,
and probably in French ones too, was so bad that
travellers who wanted to read used candle reading

lamps, candles for the purpose were for sale on the station bookstalls. But the child's ecstatic joy and pleasure at seeing her mother, and probably a wan face and rings under her eyes from too much crying, must have touched Sarah Nesbit's heart, and she was always a most affectionate mother, so she decided, against her better judgment, to take the child with them. E. Nesbit, writing of that departure, says:

'With what delicious thrills of anticipation and excitement I packed my doll's clothes on the eve of our journey! I had a little tin trunk with a real padlock; I have it still, by the way, only now it holds old letters and a bunch of violets, and a few other little worthless things that I do not often have the courage to look at nowadays. It is battered now and the paint is worn off; but then it was fresh and shiny and I packed all the doll's clothes in it with a light heart.

'I don't remember anything about our leaving home, or saying good-bye to the boys; so I fancy that they must have gone back to school some time before; but I remember the night passage from Newhaven to Dieppe far too vividly to care to describe it. I was a very worn-out little girl indeed when we reached Rouen and 1 lay for the first time in a little white French bed.'

From Rouen the party moved to Paris, from there to Tours, and from there to Poitiers, and from there to Bordeaux, where the over-imaginative child suffered the worst fright of her fright-ridden childhood, which was the more acute because, already homesick, she had hoped to recreate England by visiting objects which she knew at home. Here is her own story of what happened:

'It was because I was tired of churches and picture-galleries, of fairs and markets, of the strange babble of foreign tongues and the thin English of the guide-book, that I begged so hard to be taken to see the mummies. To me the name of a mummy was as a friend's name. As one Englishman travelling across a desert seeks to find another of whom he has heard in that far land, so I sought to meet these mummies who had cousins at home, in the British Museum, in dear, dear England.

'My fancy did not paint mummies for me apart from plate-glass cases, camphor, boarded galleries, and kindly curators, and I longed to see them as I longed to see home, and to hear my own tongue spoken about me.

'I was consumed by a fever of impatience for the three days which had to go by before the coming of the day on which the treasures might be visited. My sisters, who were to lead me to these delights, believed too that the mummies would be chiefly interesting on account of their association with Bloomsbury.

'Well, we went – I in my best blue silk frock, which I insisted on wearing to honour the occasion, holding the hand of my sister and positively skipping with delicious anticipation. There was some delay about keys, during which my excitement was scarcely to be restrained. Then we went through an arched door-way and along a flagged passage, the old man who guided us explaining volubly in French as we went.

'"What does he say?"

'"He says they are natural mummies."

'"What does that mean?"

'"They are not embalmed by man, like the Egyptian ones, but simply by the peculiar earth of the church-yard where they were buried."

'The words did not touch my conception of the glass cases and their good-natured guardian.

'The passage began to slope downward. A chill air breathed on our faces, bringing with it a deep earthy smell. Then we came to some narrow stone steps. Our guide spoke again.

'"What does he say?"

'"We are to be careful, the steps are slippery and mouldy."

'I think even then my expectation still was of a long clean gallery, filled with the white light of a London noon, shed through high skylights on Egyptian treasures. But the stairs were dark, and I held my sister's hand tightly. Down we went, down, down!

'"What does he say?"

'"We are under the church now; these are the vaults."

'We went along another passage, the damp mouldy smell increasing, and my clasp of my sister's hand grew closer and closer.

'We stopped in front of a heavy door barred with iron, and our guide turned a big reluctant key in a lock that grated . . .

'"*Les voilà*," he said, throwing open the door and drawing back dramatically.

'The vision of dry boards and white light and glass cases vanished, and in its stead I saw this:

'A small vault, as my memory serves me, about fifteen feet square, with an arched roof, from the centre of which hung a lamp that burned with a faint blue light, and made the guide's candle look red and lurid. The floor was flagged like the passages, and was as damp and chill. Round three sides of the room ran a railing, and behind it – standing against the wall, with a ghastly look of life in death – were about two hundred skeletons. Not white clean skeletons, hung on wires, like the one you see at the doctor's, but skeletons with the flesh hardened on their bones, with their long dry hair hanging on each side of their brown faces, where the skin in drying had drawn itself back from their gleaming teeth and empty eye-sockets. Skeletons draped in mouldering shreds of shrouds and grave-clothes, their lean fingers still clothed with dry skin, seemed to reach out towards me. There they stood, men, women, and children, knee-deep in loose bones collected from the other vaults of the church, and heaped round them. On the wall near the door I saw the dried body of a little child hung up by its hair.

'I don't think I screamed or cried, or even said a word. I think I was paralysed with horror, but I remember presently going back up those stairs, holding tightly to that kindly hand, and not daring to turn my head lest one of those charnel-house faces should peep out at me from some niche in the damp wall.

'It must have been late afternoon, and in the hurry of dressing for the table d'hôte my stupor of fright must have passed unnoticed, for the next thing I remember is being alone in a large room, waiting as usual for my supper to be sent up. For my mother did not approve of late dinners for little people, and I was accustomed to have bread-and-milk alone while she and my sisters dined.

'It was a large room, and very imperfectly lighted by the two wax candles in silver candlesticks. There were two windows and a curtained alcove, where the beds were. Suddenly my blood ran cold. What was behind that curtain? Beds. "Yes," whispered something that was I, and yet not I; "but suppose there are no beds there now. Only mummies, mummies, mummies!"

'A sudden noise; I screamed with terror. It was only the door opening to let the waiter in. He was a young waiter, hardly more than a boy, and had always smiled kindly at me when we met, though hitherto our intercourse had not gone farther. Now I rushed to him and flung my arms round him, to his intense amazement and the near ruin of my bread-and-milk. He spoke no English and I no French, but somehow he managed to understand that I was afraid, and afraid of that curtained alcove.

'He set down the break-and-milk, and he took me in his arms and together we fetched more candles, and then he drew back the awful curtain, and showed me the beds lying white and quiet. If I could have spoken French I should have said:

'"Yes; but how do I know it was all like that just now, before you drew the curtain?"

'As it was I said nothing, only clung to his neck.

'I hope he did not get into any trouble that night for neglected duties, for he did not attempt to leave me till my mother came back. He sat down with me on his knee and petted me and sang to me under his breath and fed me with the bread-and-milk, when by-and-by I grew calm enough to take it. All good things be with him wherever he is! I like best to think of him in a little hotel of his own, a quiet little country inn standing back from a straight road bordered with apple trees and poplars. There are wooden benches outside the door, and within a white-washed kitchen, where a plump rosy-faced woman is busy with many cares – never busy enough, however, to pass the master of the house without a loving word or a loving look. I like to believe that now he has little children

D

of his own, who hold out their arms when he opens
the door, and who climb upon his knees clamouring,
for those same songs which he sang, out of the kindness of his boyish heart, to the little frightened
English child, such a long, long time ago.'

It is not however the description of the visit to the
mummies or the kindness of the waiter, which for E.
Nesbit lovers makes that experience so fascinating,
but her summing up of it:

'The mummies of Bordeaux were the crowning
horror of my childish life; it is to them, I think, more
than to any other thing, that I owe nights and nights
of anguish and horror, long years of bitterest fear and
dread. All the other fears could have been effaced, but
the shock of that sight branded it on my brain, and I
never forgot it. For many years I could not bring
myself to go about any house in the dark, and long
after I was a grown woman I was tortured, in the
dark watches, by imagination and memory, who rose
strong and united, overpowering my will and my
reason as utterly as in my baby days.
    'It was not till I had two little children of my own
that I was able to conquer this mortal terror of darkness, and teach imagination her place, under the foot
of reason and will.
    'My children, I resolved, should never know such
fear. And to guard them from it I must banish it from
my own soul. It was not easy, but it was done. It is
banished now, and my babies, thank God, never have
known it. It was a dark cloud that overshadowed my
childhood, and I don't believe my mother ever knew
how dark it was, for I could not tell anyone the full
horror of it while it was over me, and when it had

passed I came from under it, as one who has lived long years in an enchanter's castle, where the sun is darkened always, might come forth into the splendour of noontide. Such a one breathes God's sweet air and beholds the free heavens with joyous leaps of heart; but he does not speak soon nor lightly of what befell in the dark, in the evil days, in the Castle of the Enchanter.'

Of course she was not able to free her own babies from fears, no mother can do that, but she almost certainly helped all her children readers to escape from their own particular enchanter's castle. There is, even in the magic books, such a wind of sanity blowing through their covers that it must have helped many children to forget what befell them in their dark hours. That is the best of being a magician.

CHAPTER FIVE

France

PERHAPS E. NESBIT'S greatest gift as a writer for children was her naturalistic amusing dialogue. With the exception of a few words she is quite undated, for she avoided to a large extent the slang of her day and used instead family expressions and words, which curiously enough so seldom find their way on to paper, although they exist in every family. But what is so odd in the Nesbit story is that she herself was not sufficiently with her brothers and sisters for a satisfactory glossary of words and phrases to have been part of her childhood. There could have been, and probably were, a number of expressions built on events, persons and objects who belonged to the Kennington Lane days. All the children would have known at once what was referred to if the expression was used 'Very emu-ish looking', and no doubt there were a mass of family jokes and expressions built round the agricultural college, but afterwards there does not seem to have been a long enough shared period of time for a library of words belonging to the Nesbits as a family to have been built up. Probably, at least for the boys and Edith, a perfect place was for ever summed up by 'it was Buckinghamshire', or some such phrase, after the much enjoyed holiday there, but for a proper family dictionary of expressions a stable background is needed, and that

E. Nesbit missed. But clearly she never forgot what family language should be, and its importance in family life, so she gave words and expressions to all her fiction families, and how right she was, for it is the family atmosphere more than perhaps any other quality that makes her books live. How splendid too are her own words picked to paint what she means, words which splash colour on to her pages. "'Three cheers for thoughtful Jane," cried Cyril, now roused at last from his yawning despair.' What better word could be used to describe a child's despair than yawning?

Having accepted that Edith was fundamentally unsuited to boarding schools, or at least to the schools she chose for her, Sarah Nesbit decided on a different form of education for the child; she should be educated with one other girl, and since they were in France, the child would be French, which would mean Edith would learn to speak French like a native. A family called Lourdes was selected, and Edith became a member of a French family and did lessons with the daughter Marguerite. She wrote a description of her life in that household, which is interesting as showing a different side to the child's character:

'She was the most beautiful person in the world. She had brown eyes and pink cheeks, a blue silk dress and a white bonnet with orange-blossoms in it. She had two pairs of shoes and two pairs of stockings, and she had two wigs, a brown and a flaxen one. All her clothes took off and on, and there was a complete change of them.

'I saw her first at a bazaar and longed to possess her, but her price was two guineas, and no hope mingled with my longing.

'Here let me make a confession, I had never really

loved any doll. My affections up to that time had been lavished on a black and white spotted penny rabbit, bought at a Kentish fair; but when I saw Renée, it seemed to me that if I could love a doll, this would be the one.

'We were at Pau then in a 'select boarding-house'. I was bored with travel, as I believe all children are – so large a part of a child's life is made up of little familiar playthings and objects; it has little of that historic and artistic sense which lends colour and delight to travel. I was tired of wandering about, and glad to think we were to stay in Pau for the winter. The bazaar pleased me. It was got up by the English residents, and their fancy-work was the fancy-work of the church bazaars in England, and I felt at home among it, and when my eyes rested on Renée I saw the most delightful object I had seen for many weeks. I looked and longed, and longed and looked, and then suddenly in a moment one of the great good fortunes of my life happened to me. The beautiful doll was put up to be raffled, and my sister won her. I trembled with joy as she and her wardrobe were put into my hands. I took her home. I dressed and undressed her twenty times a day. I made her play the part of heroine in all my favourite stories. I told her fairy-tales and took her to bed with me at night for company, but I never loved her. I have never been able to love a doll in my life.

'My mother came to me the next day as I was changing Renée's wig, and said, "Don't you think it's almost time that you began to have some lessons again; I don't want my little girl to grow up quite ignorant, you wouldn't like that yourself, would you?"

'"I don't know," I said doubtfully, feeling that

ignorance in a grown-up state was surely to be preferred to a return to Stamford and long division.

'"I am not going to send you to school," my mother hastened to add, doubtless seeing the cloud that gathered in my face. "I know a French lady here who has a little girl about your age, and she says that you can go and live with her for a while and learn French."

'"Is she a nice little girl?" I asked. "What is she like?"

'"Well, she's rather like your new doll," my mother laughed, "when it has the flaxen wig on. Think how nice it will be to be able to write letters home in French."

'I knew Miss — could not write letters in French, and the prospect of crushing her with my new literary attainment filled my wicked little heart.

'"I should like to go and live with the little girl who is like my new dollie," I said, "if you will come and see me every day."

'So I went, my doll's clothes packed in their little tin trunk. And I stood stealing shy side-glances at Marguerite, who was certainly very like my doll, while my mother and her mother were exchanging last civilities. I was so pleased with the new surroundings, the very French interior, the excitement of being received as a member by a real French family, that I forgot to cry till the wheels of my mother's carriage had rolled away from the door.

'Then I was left, a little English child without a word of French in the bosom of a French family, and as this came upon me I burst into a flood of tears.

'Madame Lourdes could speak no English but she knew the universal language, the language of love and kindness.

'She drew me to her ample lap, wiped my eyes,

smiled at me and chattered volubly in her own tongue words whose sense was dead to me, but whose tone breathed of tenderness and sympathy. By the time Mlle. Lourdes, the only English-speaking member of the family came home from her daily round of teaching, Marguerite and I were unpacking my doll's clothes together and were laughing at our vain efforts to understand each other.

'I learned French in three months. All day I was with Madame Lourdes or Marguerite, neither of whom knew a word of English. It was French or silence, and any healthy child would have chosen French, as I did. They were three happy months. I adored Marguerite who was, I think, the typical good child of the French story-books. She wore her hair in a little yellow plait down her back.

'I do not think we ever got into wilful mischief. For instance, our starving the cat was quite unintentional. We were playing bandits in a sort of cellar that opened from the triangular courtyard in front of the house and it occurred to us that Mimi would make an excellent captive princess, so we caught her and put her in a hamper at the end of the cellar, and when my mother called to take us home to tea with her, we rushed off and left the poor princess still a prisoner. If we hadn't been out that evening we must have been reminded of her existence by the search for her, but Madame Lourdes, failing to find the cat, concluded that she must have run away or met with an accident, and did not mention the matter to us out of consideration for our feelings, so that it was not till two nights later that I started up in bed about midnight and pulled Marguerite's yellow pigtail wildly.

'"Oh, Marguerite," I cried, "poor Mimi!" I had to

pull at the pigtail as though it was a bell-rope, and I had pulled three times before I could get Marguerite to understand what was the matter with me. Then she sat up in bed rigid with a great purpose. "We must go down and fetch her," she said.

'It was winter; the snow was on the ground. Marguerite thoughtfully put on her shoes and her dressing-gown, but I, with some vague recollection of bare-footed pilgrims, and some wild desire to make expiation for my crime, went down bare-footed, in my night-gown. The crime of forgetting a cat for three days was well paid for by that expedition. We crept through the house like mice; across the courtyard, thinly sprinkled with snow, and into that awful black yawning cellar where nameless horrors lurked behind each bit of shapeless lumber, ready to leap out upon us as we passed. Marguerite did not share my terrors. She only remarked that it was very cold and that we must make haste. We opened the hamper fully expecting to find the captive dead, and my heart gave a leap of delight when, as we raised the lid, the large white Mimi crept out and began to rub herself against us with joyous purrings. I remember so well the feeling of her soft warm fur against my cold little legs. I caught the cat in my arms, and as I turned to go back to the house my half-frozen foot struck against something on the floor. It felt silky, I picked it up. It was Renée. She also had been a captive princess in our game of bandits. She also had been shut up here all this time, and I had never missed her!

'We took the cat and the doll back to bed with us and tried to get warm again. Marguerite was soon asleep, but I lay awake for a long time kissing and crying over the ill-used cat.

'I didn't get up again for a fortnight. My bare-footed pilgrimage cost me a frightful cold and the loss of several children's parties to which we had been invited. Marguerite, throughout my illness, behaved like an angel.

'I only remember one occasion on which I quarrelled with her – it was on the subject of dress. We were going to a children's party and my best blue silk was put out for me to wear.

'"I wish you wouldn't wear that," said Marguerite hesitatingly, "it makes my grey cashmere look so old."

'Now I had nothing else to wear but a brown frock which I hated.

'"Never mind,' I said hypocritically, "it's better to be good than smart, everybody says so," and I put on my blue silk. When I was dressed, I pranced off to the kitchen to show my finery to the cook, and under her admiring eyes executed my best curtsey. It began, of course, by drawing the right foot back; it ended in a tub of clothes and water that was standing just behind me. I floundered out somehow, and my first thought was how funny I must have looked, and in another moment I should have burst out laughing, but as I scrambled out, I saw Marguerite in the doorway, smiling triumphantly, and heard her thin little voice say, "The blue silk can't mock the poor grey cashmere now!"

'An impulse of blind fury came upon me. I caught Marguerite by her little shoulders, and before the cook could interfere I had ducked her head-first into the tub of linen. Madame Lourdes behaved beautifully; she appeared on the scene at this moment, and, impartial as ever, she slapped us both, but when she heard from the cook the rights of the story, my sentence was "bed". "But Marguerite," said her mother, "has been punished enough for an unkind word."

'And Marguerite was indeed sobbing bitterly, while I was dry-eyed and still furious. "She can't go," I cried, "she hasn't got a dress!"

'"You have spoilt her dress," said Madame Lourdes coolly, "the least you can do is to lend her your brown one." And that excellent woman actually had the courage to send her own daughter to a party in my dress, an exquisite punishment to us both.

'Marguerite came to my bedside that night; she had taken off the brown dress and wore her little flannel dressing-gown.

'"You're not cross now, are you?" she said. "I did beg mother to let you come, and I've not enjoyed myself a bit, and I've brought you this from the party."

'It was a beautiful little model of a coffee mill made in sugar. My resentment could not withstand this peace-offering. I never quarrelled with Marguerite again, and when my mother sent for me to join her at Bagnères I wept as bitterly at leaving Madame Lourdes as I had done at being left with her.

'"Cheer up my darling, my cabbage," said the dear woman as the tears stood in her own little grey eyes. "I have an instinct, a presentiment, which tells me we shall meet again."

But she never did meet Marguerite again, that was a feature of the childhood that she said was no different to that of other children. She had no roots, she never knew what happened to Marguerite, or Mimi the cat, any more than she knew what happened to the nice waiter or the horrible Stuart plaid, she was always moving on. In *The Story of the Amulet* she

describes the unlived-in feeling of lodgings, where you
were always a stranger to the furniture.

'Old Nurse had been in the habit of letting lodgings,
till Father gave her the children to take care of. And
her rooms were furnished "for letting". Now it is a
very odd thing that no one ever seems to furnish a
room "for letting" in a bit the same way as one would
furnish it for living in. This room had heavy dark red
stuff curtains – the colour that blood would not make
a stain on – with coarse lace curtains inside. The carpet was yellow, and violet, with bits of grey and brown
oilcloth in odd places. The fireplace had shavings and
tinsel in it. There was a very varnished mahogany
chiffonier, or sideboard, with a lock that wouldn't
act. There were hard chairs – far too many of them –
with crochet antimacassars slipping off their seats,
all of which sloped the wrong way. The table wore a
cloth of a cruel green colour with a yellow chain-
stitch pattern round it. Over the fireplace was a look-
ing-glass that made you look much uglier than you
really were, however plain you might be to begin with.
Then there was a mantel-board with maroon plush
and wool fringe that did not match the plush; a
dreary clock like a black marble tomb – it was silent
as the grave too, for it had long since forgotten how
to tick. And there were painted glass vases that never
had any flowers in, and a painted tambourine that no
one ever played, and painted brackets with nothing
on them.'

The affinity between Old Nurse's lodging and the
pensions of her childhood is shown by something
Nesbit wrote about the days immediately following
her return from the Lourdes family. The Nesbits at

the time were living in a pension at Bagnères de Bigorre.

'The excitement of coming back to my mother had quickly worn off. My mother was busy letter-writing, so were my sisters. I missed Marguerite, Mimi, even my lessons. There was something terribly unhome-like about the polished floor, the polished wooden furniture, the marble-topped chests of drawers with glass handles, and the cold greyness of the stone-built houses outside. I wandered about the suite of apartments, every now and then rubbing myself like a kitten against my mother's shoulder and murmuring, "I don't know what to do." I tried drawing, but the pencil was bad and the paper greasy. I thought of reading, but there was no book there I cared for. It was one of the longest days I ever spent.'

All Nesbit's fiction children knew days which were longer than imagining could have invented, and 'What shall we do?' brought nothing to the mind. A situation so admirably summed up by Anthea on the first fearful day in Old Nurse's lodgings when she said, speaking for all bored children everywhere, 'Don't let's think about how horrid it all is. I mean we can't go to things that cost a lot, but we must do *something*.' And Cyril, Robert, Anthea and Jane being children of Nesbit's mind, of course not only did *something* but a wildly exciting *something*. In concocting the *something* did E. Nesbit throw a smile over her shoulder to the small bored child in the pension at Bagnères de Bigorre, for whom, on one occasion at least, nothing happened at all?

CHAPTER SIX

Germany and Halstead

A FEATURE of E. Nesbit's children's books which makes her almost unique amongst children's writers is that her boys are as well drawn, sometimes better drawn than her girls. Few indeed have been the women writers of whom that could be said, or indeed vice versa, few are the men writers whose girls are as well drawn as their boys.

The answer in E. Nesbit's case is undoubtedly her brothers, Alfred and Henry. Holidays she describes in much-loved houses were made perfect because her brothers were there, for when Alfred and Henry were about, her life, otherwise rather solitary, for much as she loved Mary the gap in years between them was too great for them to be playmates, became full of adventure.

From everything that she writes about them Alfred and Henry must have been exceptionally nice brothers, willing in fact, apparently pleased to have a small sister tagging along with them which many brothers are not. And though of course in the haze that hangs over things remembered, it is likely the good comradeship shines out and the days when she was not wanted are forgotten, yet without doubt there was a very strong bond between the brothers and their little sister, shown in the words that she wrote already quoted, about the summer in the house outside Dinan: 'My brothers eagerly led me round to show me all the treasures of the new house.' It is unlikely that her memory played her false about that welcome and 'eagerly' was the word that came to her mind.

But the bond between E. Nesbit and her brothers was most clearly shown when she was at school in Germany. While Sarah Nesbit made her home outside Dinan Edith had attended two schools. The first was kept by a Mademoiselle Faucet, and the second was an Ursuline Convent. It was while she was at this convent, aged about eleven, that she seems to have developed as a personality. She was to grow up to be an artist, and must already have felt the need to express herself, and not finding an outlet, apparently went through a patch, not unusual in children who are to be artists, of 'bustin' out all over' like spring in the song in *Carousel*. She was all her life to have a fiery temper, and she was always to be over-emotional, so of course with adolescence round the corner these faults became more pronounced, and her need to express herself probably led her into excesses of every sort: of love, of hate, of outward show, of grief, all symptomatic, if only she was understood, of the stirrings in the chrysalis made by the exotic butterfly which would some day emerge. Whether Sarah Nesbit understood or not she was probably anxious about her youngest daughter, who was so different from Saretta or from Mary, both so much easier to raise, for it is hard for a mother to remember while a stormy petrel of a child is growing up that the good and placid child is unlikely to be the one to bring fame to the family. Anyway, whatever the reason, Sarah Nesbit thought that it was time Edith was moved from the Ursuline Convent, and the Mother

Superior probably agreed with her, so she and her brothers were sent to schools in Germany.

As so often happened, Sarah Nesbit was unlucky in the school that she picked, which was particularly unfortunate as the child, not yet twelve, was so far from home. She loathed the German school, and acquired a detestation of all things German, which lasted throughout her life. She wrote a couple of lines of verse at that school which sums up her feelings:

> 'God! Let the Germans be suppressed
> So that Europe at last may have a rest!'

Edith was, as we know, a nervous child, a prey to every sort of imaginary fear, yet her dislike of the German school was so strong that it overrode her fears. It is enough to frighten an adult to be alone and penniless in a foreign country, especially if it is a country you already fear and hate, yet Edith, not yet twelve, was brave enough to attempt to run away three times, and the last time she succeeded in trying to reach her brothers. She has not unfortunately written of that experience, but she talked of it to her children. She did not know her way about the German countryside, so had no means of finding her brothers' school, so she spent her day of liberty cowering in a field. Hunger forced the child to return to her school, in what agony of mind can only be imagined. To return at all to the loathed place was hard enough, but to have the one thing that kept her courage alive taken from her, that was the heart of suffering, for she could no longer believe that if only she was brave enough to run away it would mean reunion with Alfred and Henry.

The Franco-Prussian war was her means of escape from the German school, for Sarah Nesbit felt she could not leave her child in a country at war, and via England she returned, apparently alone, for oddly enough Alfred and Henry do not appear to have travelled with her, to Dinan.

That same year Sarah Nesbit, probably because France was at war, at last brought her family home to England. She purchased a house in Kent, a house which to E. Nesbit was the most loved of all her homes, partly because it was in England, but also because it was permanent, and she was old enough to appreciate everything about it.

'After many wanderings my mother took a house at Halstead, "The Hall" it was called, but the house itself did not lend itself to the pretensions of its name. A long, low, red-brick house, that might have been commonplace but for the roses and ivy that clung to the front of it, and the rich, heavy jasmine that covered the side. There was a smooth lawn with chestnut trees round it, and a big garden, where flowers and fruit and vegetables grew together, as they should, without jealousy or class-distinction. There never were such peonies as grew among our currant-bushes, nor such apricots as hung among the leaves on the sunny south wall. From a laburnum tree in a corner of the lawn we children slung an improvised hammock, and there I used to read and dream, and watch the swaying green gold of leaf and blossom.

'Our garden ran round three sides of a big pond. Perhaps it was true that the pond did not make the house more healthy. It certainly made it more interesting. Besides the raft (which was but a dull thing when the boys were away at school), there were nooks among the laburnums and lilacs that grew thickly round the pond, nooks where one could hide with

E

one's favourite books, and be secure from the insistent and irritating demands so often made on one's time by one's elders. For grown-up people never thought of spoiling their clothes by penetrating the shrubbery. Here, on many a sunny day, have I lounged away the morning, stifling conscience with Mrs. Ewing's tales, and refusing to remember the tangle of untidiness in which I had left my room involved.'

'Which was but a dull thing when the boys were away at school,' those brothers, who in a second could turn that pond into the Pacific, the Zambesi, or the Caribbean, on which the raft was adrift, something beyond a girl on her own. Those brothers who had only to come into a house to make it their place, who made it impossible for their youngest sister to be bored or dull. It is no wonder that when she began to write for children it was boys E. Nesbit first thought of, boys who had the ideas and got things going, so she invented her Bastable family.

J. B. Priestley, in an appreciation of the E. Nesbit books on her death for the 1924 of *The Bookman*, wrote that 'it was a pleasant change to say the least of it, to see life from the small boys' angle of vision'. This was written about *The Bastables*, but he admitted a preference for the magic books, for the adventures of Jane, Anthea, Robert and Cyril, and most of all for Jerry, Jimmy and Kathleen of *The Enchanted Castle*, about which he wrote that this was 'perhaps her best all-round story'. Nesbit lovers are bound to be divided as to which is her best book and which her most lovable family, and few of them would omit Bobby, Peter and Phyllis of *The Railway Children*, as did J. B. Priestley in that appreciation. But Priestley was writing in 1924 for the Christmas number of '*The*

Bookman, and E. Nesbit had only died the previous May, so it was too early to judge her books as classics, for no books are admitted to be classics in the author's lifetime. Now we can see that the books must not be judged one against the other, but against all books written for children both past and present, and on that count they come out very high on the list. In the special *Sunday Times Survey* held at the end of 1957 to discover the hundred best books for children, written in English or translated into it, which were in print, E. Nesbit was one of the six whose name appears twice, the others were Mark Twain, Charles Kingsley, Rudyard Kipling (three of his books were chosen), Robert Louis Stevenson, and Walter de la Mare, glittering companions indeed.

To get anywhere near to assessing the Nesbit magic and how she achieved it, a first step is to try and know her children as she knew them. We begin with the Bastables.

CHAPTER SEVEN

The Bastables

THE BASTABLES, as their fans know, appear in three books, *The Story of the Treasure Seekers*, *The Wouldbegoods*, and the *New Treasure Seekers*. There are those who swear the Bastable children are E. Nesbit's finest creations, but she is one of the fortunate amongst writers in that she wrote many good books, so that her name need not be linked with one title or group of titles by which all her other work must be judged.

Being Nesbit she gives the Bastables a house to live in before she introduces her family. They lived, when first met, in a semi-detached house in Lewisham, which had a small garden at the back which was presumably allowed to run wild, for a visiting gardener only tidied the bit in front. There was one general servant, of whom Oswald said: 'A great deal of your comfort and happiness depends on having a good general.' The one when the story begins was not good, for she always made sago puddings – 'the watery kind, and you cannot pretend anything with them, not even islands, like you do with porridge.'

The house in the Lewisham Road when first seen is a dreary down-at-heel place, for the carpets were in holes, and when the legs came off things they were not sent to be mended, for money was terribly scarce. But, though it does not sound likely, it must have

68

been a nice house once, for Oswald remembered it in the days when there were several servants, and the house and garden were kept as they should be, and people came to dinner driving in cabs, the women wearing pretty dresses.

Poverty, and it was down-to-the-bone, genteel poverty which the Bastables endured, is something about which E. Nesbit wrote, which did not belong to her childhood. Even after her father's death her mother was comfortably off, but she knew poverty from first-hand as a young married woman. Her husband Hubert Bland, who had been a bank clerk, had, as already mentioned invested all his money in a small business which had barely got going when he was taken desperately ill with smallpox, and when, after several relapses, he struggled back to health it was to find his partner had absconded with all the money in the business. E. Nesbit, with babies and a husband to support, managed to keep the home going and the wolf on the doorstep, rather than in residence, by writing stories, and reciting for fees. She was very young at the time, and troubles can roll off the backs of the young, but the poverty of those days she never forgot, as her books for children testify; to the Bastables she even gave a similar house to the one she had struggled so hard to maintain, for her home too was in the Lewisham Road.

Probably because she had lost her father when she was tiny, E. Nesbit's children never live at home with both parents. The Bastable children's mother is dead, and although all three books about the family are immensely amusing, and packed with adventures, never does E. Nesbit let her readers forget that the children miss their mother desperately, and try if possible not to think about her, or even about other people's mothers, because they know if they do that a wave of misery, which could swamp even their spirits, is waiting to engulf them.

'Our mother is dead, and if you think we don't care because I don't tell you much about her you only show that you do not understand people at all.' Oswald wrote at the beginning of *The Story of the Treasure Seekers*. And in the *New Treasure Seekers*:

'We had not seen the sea since before Mother died. I believe we older ones all thought of that, and it made us quieter than the younger ones were. I do not want to forget anything, but it makes you feel empty and stupid when you remember some things.'

And Alice in *The Story of the Treasure Seekers*, apologising for kidnapping Albert-next-door: 'We're very, very sorry. We didn't think about his mother. You see we try very hard not to think about other people's mothers because . . .'

Or Oswald on Christmas. 'It was Christmas, nearly a year after Mother died. I cannot write about Mother – but I will just say one thing. If she had only been away for a little while, and not for always, we shouldn't have been so keen on having a Christmas. I didn't understand this then, but I am much older now, and I think it was just because everything was so different and horrid we felt we *must* do something; and perhaps we were not particular enough *what*. Things make you much more unhappy when you loaf about than when you are doing events.'

So all the way through the books, without Oswald saying much about her, Mother, who had made home home, who would have understood even the deepest trouble her family got into, whose memory has to be pushed into the background if lumps in the throat are to be avoided, is on every page.

One way of gauging the aliveness of a family in a children's book is to ask yourself: 'Would I know them, if they sat opposite to me in a bus?' The answer in the best family books is invariably 'yes'. Who could fail to know the March girls, not individually but as a group? Or to take a modern example, who could miss The Ruggles of One End Street? The Bastables would not have time to sit down before everyone who knew them would be whispering 'Look who's here'. Dora, rather anxious, either carrying the fares or making sure Oswald has them, looking nervously at the family to be sure they are behaving suitably, and swinging round every time the bus stops to be sure she has not passed her destination. Oswald, lolling back in his seat, his eyes shining for the bus has ceased to be a bus, and his destination is none of those of which the bus conductor has heard. Dicky, as Oswald described him, 'angel-like and innocent-looking'. Noël and Alice probably recognizable as twins, and Noël certainly recognizable by his fragility, and possibly by a cough, and perhaps a narrow chest. And little H. O. swinging his legs and insisting on his right to do something or other. The whole family desperately shabby and, in spite of Dora's efforts, in need of patching, mending, and all the other attentions they would have had if their mother were still alive.

E. Nesbit has perhaps been a little unfair to Dora. She was not intended to be a vivid personality, but there was good in the girl, and it is tough on her that she had only Oswald to speak for her, since to him she appeared so often to be a blight on the pleasures of others. But considering Dora as she was, it is impossible not to feel sorry for her. We know because Dora told Oswald so, that her mother before she died gave her brothers and sister into her care: 'Dora, take care of the others, and teach them to be good, and keep them out of trouble and make them happy.' And, poor girl, how hard she tried to do these things, but in books, as in life, such admirable efforts, however well-meant, can to others seem tiresome.

Dora, when we first meet her, must have been thirteen or even fourteen, for Oswald and Dicky came between her and the twins, who were ten, an awkward age, at one moment stepping away from childhood, and at another stepping back into it, so that she can be found throwing cares aside and saying at one minute: 'Let's try my way *now*. Besides, I'm the eldest, so it's only fair. Let's dig for treasure. Not any tiresome divining-rod – but just plain digging. People who dig for treasure always find it.' And the next moment refusing to sit in a makeshift tent made of blankets off the family beds, and the kitchen clothes-horse, because she is going in a grown-up way to look at the shops.

It is to be supposed that Dora and Alice could look pretty, for Oswald reporting on the marriage of Albert-next-door's Uncle, and his long lost love, stated that his sisters as bridesmaids 'didn't look so bad, though rather as if they were in a Christmas card', which is high praise, as E. Nesbit knew, from a brother. There is actually only one other occasion on which Oswald speaks in a completely complimentary way of Dora, and that was when Dicky sent the booby-trap hamper to the porter who refused to let him climb into a moving train; the affair it will be remembered, finished in a real hamper of good things having to be provided, eventually paid for out of pocket money, and of this Oswald reports: 'Dora paid her share, too, though she wasn't in it. The author does not shrink from owning that this was very decent of Dora.'

Although Oswald had no difficulty in finding nice things to say about Alice, the girls in the Bastable family are not as vividly drawn as the boys. All authors have difficulty now and then in restraining a character who gets the bit between his or her teeth, as it were, and dashes off disregarding the author's hands on the reins. Such a character Oswald undoubtedly was. E. Nesbit, much as she longed to recreate her brothers, cannot originally have intended Oswald to hog so much of her stories, but who, having created an Oswald, could bear to curtail him in any way?

What do the readers know of Alice? As already mentioned, she was ten, and Noël's twin, but Noël absolutely refuses to allow Oswald to diminish his importance, which Alice, by nature a self-effacing child, does permit. She was a child with a social sense. It was she who felt so acutely the shame of the plum pudding spurned by the poor person, that Oswald writes: 'Alice, the most paralysed with disgrace of all of us . . .'

At a guess Alice must have been drawn on E. Nesbit's memory of herself at the age of ten, for she is so in everything with the boys. When defending the aged Eastern, Oswald reporting the fight with the boy bullies, wrote: 'The battle raged, and Alice often turned the tide of it by a well-timed shove or nip.' And when the aged Eastern's wife rewarded Alice with a parrot and she shared its ownership with Oswald and Dicky, Oswald pays her the highest compliment at his command: 'She is tremendously straight. I often wonder why she was made a girl. She's a jolly sight more of a gentleman than half the boys at our school.'

But at the time of which Nesbit was writing girls, even the best of them, were always very feminine and burst into tears on the slightest provocation, so that on that same occasion Oswald had to write: 'Alice had burst out crying and was howling as though she would never stop. That is the worst of girls – they never can keep anything up. Any brave act they may suddenly do, when for a moment they forget that they have not the honour to be boys, is almost instantly made into contemptibility by a sudden attack of crybabyishness.'

But in spite of her being a weak female, it was often Alice who had the most unfortunate well-intended ideas. It was she, it will be remembered, who thought up the scheme to help the bargee. 'Then Alice said, "They have gone to find the man who turns on the water to fill the pen. I dare say they won't find him. He's gone to his dinner, I shouldn't wonder. What a lovely surprise it would be if they came back to find their barge floating high and dry on a lot of water!"'

And it was Alice who said, looking at the stream in the orchard: 'Why not go and discover the source of the Nile?' An affair which ended in a burnt bridge, and a dam which ruined seven pounds' worth of barley.

Perhaps the best summing up of Alice is in the *New Treasure Seekers*, where Oswald states: 'Everybody is always wanting to kiss Alice.'

Of the boys the most difficult to know is Dicky, because being next in age to Oswald he took a major part in most of the adventures with Oswald, but Oswald of course mainly reports on himself. Dicky, when first met, must have been about eleven. He is recorded as being good at sums, and his father called him the Definite Article, because he wanted everything settled exactly. E. Nesbit must have given much thought to the character of Dicky when she was planning her Bastable family, for he is splendidly imagined to show up the unusualness of Oswald, and is a good contrast to Noël. E. Nesbit would not have needed to consider H. O. in relation to his brothers, because as the little boy of the party he stands on his own.

Dicky is exactly the leavening the Bastables as a fiction family need. He is not so easily carried away, he thinks before he does things, he even on occasion looks far enough ahead to see consequences, so much so that Oswald wrote of Dicky: 'He really has not the proper soul for adventures.' True, on that occasion Dicky had been sea-sick all night, so that Oswald added: '. . . and what soul he has had been damped by what he had gone through.'

But though he had not as proper a soul for adventures as Oswald, Dicky was the member of the family to come out with the unvarnished, unacceptable truth, and so was invaluable to E. Nesbit. '*That's* cheating,' said Dicky, 'downright beastly, mean, low cheating.' Or when wedding presents that might have been given to Albert-next-door's Uncle were under discussion, and Oswald said, 'I've sometimes wished we'd given Albert's uncle a really truly present that we'd chosen ourselves and bought with our own chink.' And Noël added: 'I'd have killed a dragon for him as soon as look at it,' Dicky silenced further foolish talk by saying: '. . . we just gave rotten books. But it's no use grizzling over it now. It's all over, and he won't get married again while she's alive.'

A sterling boy Dicky.

Noël is a delicious character, after Oswald probably E. Nesbit's favourite, for though authors, like parents, should not have favourites in their families, few authors seem able to avoid this failing. E. Nesbit wrote verse as a child, and in her teens it was her main leisure-time occupation. She had in The Hall at Halstead a room of her own, of which she wrote:

'Here I wrote and dreamed, and never showed my verses or told my dreams for many a long month. But when I was fifteen I ventured to show some verses to my mother. She showed them to Mr. Japp, then editor of *Good Words* and *The Sunday Magazine,* and never shall I forget the rapture of delight and of gratitude with which I received the news that my verses had been accepted. By-and-by they were printed, and I got a cheque for a guinea – a whole guinea, think of it! Now the day when I should be a poet seemed almost at hand. Had I not had a poem printed?'

To Noël she entrusted her own creature urge, and to Noël she gave the same happiness by allowing him to earn a guinea, and to know the rapture of having a poem printed. Because she had made Noël only ten she was perhaps a little unkind to his poetic efforts; many small children write exquisite verse as naturally as a bird sings, whereas Noël, as sincere a poet as ever breathed, was made to write lines only to be laughed at by those who read them:

'This is the story of Agincourt.
    If you don't know it you jolly well ought.
  It was a famous battle fair,
      And all your ancestors fought there.
'That is if you come of a family old.
      The Bastables do; they were always very bold.
          And at Agincourt
          They fought
          As they ought;
          So we have been taught.'

It was probably her fear of writing verse too well

and in too sophisticated a way for someone of ten that made her allow Noël no talent, for certainly anything approaching genius would have been shockingly out of place in the Bastable family.

Noël was the family romantic; when all kinds of adventurous ideas for restoring the fortunes of the ancient House of Bastable are afoot, it was Noël who could not make up his mind whether he would print his poetry in a book and sell it, or find a Princess and marry her as his method of making money. Though he did not marry her, Noël did find a Princess, and when she asked him who he was, he replied without thought: 'I'm Prince Camaralzaman,' a most satisfactory reply, for the Princess knew she must not talk to commoners. And when the adventure was over, and the Bastables back in the Lewisham Road eating dripping toast for tea, Noël still thought affectionately of his Princess: 'I wish I could give *her* some!' he said, referring to the dripping toast, 'It is very good.' No romantic grown-up could have paid his lady a higher compliment.

Noël was very uncomplaining about his miserable health. When he caught the cold that Dicky had tried to catch, all he said was: 'You should have caught it yourself, then it wouldn't have come to me.' And when the family were crossing the river to 'where the Chinamen live', and Noël who even before the voyage had, according to Oswald, begun to look like a young throstle – all eyes and beak – was seasick, how calmly he took his fate.

'Noël pulled Alice's sleeve and said –
'"Do I look very green?"
'"You do rather, dear," she said kindly.
'"I feel much greener than I look," said Noël. And later he was not at all well.'

And yet he clearly had cause to be very sorry for himself indeed, for later in the voyage Alice said:

'Oswald, I think Noël will die if we don't make land soon.'

The youngest members of a fiction family are of immense service to their author for they can mix themselves up in affairs which even the most scatter-brained elder brothers and sisters would know should be eschewed, if retribution is not to follow. So it is poor Noël whom the unpleasant Archibald talked into cutting the water pipe with a chisel, and Noël assisted by H. O. who, believing the house to be about to be blown up by dynamite, cut the wires of the new electric light system.

But though Noël can do silly things, and because of his poetry and bronchitis is always slightly set apart from the rest of the family, he can on occasion be the family conscience. Perhaps in all the adventures E. Nesbit gave to her Bastables, none is more revealing than the chapter called 'The Turk in Chains' in the *New Treasure Seekers*. It was natural that Dicky, full of venom at missing The Hippodrome, could conceive the idea of sending the booby-trap hamper, and that for a time his enthusiasm for his joke could carry along his family with him, for poor though the Bastables had been they had never known real poverty, the sort that means going hungry. It was in fact the sort of revenge that children at any date might plan, for there was no reason for the Bastables to imagine a young wife and an old father, and times so hard that the arrival of the hamper seemed like a miracle. But E. Nesbit, knowing her Bastables, allowed one con-science to speak before the cruelty of what they had done was known to the children. Dicky, still glowing at the thought of his well-planned revenge, said: 'It *was* a ripping idea! I'm glad I thought of it!' When Noël answered:

'I'm not. I wish you hadn't – I wish we hadn't. I know just exactly what he feels like now. He feels as if he'd like to *kill* you for it, and I dare say he would if you hadn't been a craven, white-feathered skulker and not signed your name.'

A brilliantly dramatic moment, and one that shows how much the author knew about Noël, that she did not tell her readers. Knowing far more about the characters they have conceived than they write down is one of the hall-marks of the great writers for children.

H. O., or to give him his full name Horace Octavius, was eight when we first get to know him. He is an uninhibited child: 'Let's be Bandits,' said H. O., 'I dare say it's wrong, but it would be fun pretending.'

'DEAR FATHER AND EVERY ONE,' he wrote when he packed himself in the dress basket, intending to reach Rome. 'I am going to be a Clown. When I am rich and reveared I will come back rolling.

Your affectionate son,
HORACE OCTAVIUS BASTABLE.'

Oswald hints that H. O. was a backward child. 'H. O. is eight years old, but he cannot tell the clock yet. Oswald could tell the clock when he was six.'

But Oswald had a mother when he was six to teach him to read the clock, which H. O. at eight has not, and E. Nesbit remembered this, and carefully did not allow Dora to do much mothering of H. O., for she wanted him exactly the way she drew him, sturdy and independent, but at hand to carry out any good ideas she had which were too foolish for the elder children, as for instance travelling to Rome in a dress basket.

An education of a sort H. O. did receive occasionally from his brothers: 'We made H. O. prick his own thumb, because he is our little brother and it is our duty to teach him to be brave.'

H.O.'s own attitude to his position in the family was to make use of it. When it suited him he was in on whatever was going on, but also when it suited him he reminded his family of his tender years. When his father delayed talking to him about hiding in the dress basket, H. O. very properly turned on the others: 'I do wish Father wouldn't put things off so. He might just as well have spoken to me this morning. And I can't see I've done anything so awful – and it's all your faults for not looking after me. Aren't I your little brother? And it's your duty to see I do what's right. You've told me so often enough.'

When somebody has to let the cat out of the bag without worrying too much about secrets, or word of honour, H. O. is always by E. Nesbit's pen to speak out.

'"The money belonged to someone else," said Dora.

'"Who?" Mrs. Bax asked,' whereupon H. O. blurted out:

'It was Miss Sandal's money – every penny.' A most useful child for any author to have around, for none of the other children could at that moment have made that clear statement.

It was a grand idea, as E. Nesbit conceived it, of the children being forced by their consciences to give away the revolting Christmas pudding they had made, and how well she describes that pudding, knowing that horrible food was certain to appeal to her readers. But, having thought of the idea, which of her family could she allow to go out and beg for money for the

I don't suppose he was used to politeness from boys

THE STORY OF THE TREASURE SEEKERS

The Uncle was very fierce indeed with the pudding

THE STORY OF THE TREASURE SEEKERS

ingredients? H. O. of course, an H. O. entirely un-repentant, able to confess without a flicker of shame to what he had done:

'"How pleased all those kind ladies and gentlemen would be if they knew *we* were the poor children they gave the shillings and sixpences and things for!"

'We all said, "*What*?" It was no moment for politeness.

'"I say," H. O. said, "they'd be glad if they knew it was us was enjoying the pudding, and not dirty little, really poor children."'

No one who has read the Bastable books could resist H. O. and the fusses his outspokenness causes. How glad E. Nesbit must have been that she had decided to have one character who was only eight and who therefore never felt 'grown-upness creeping inordiously upon him.'

So that leaves Oswald, but as he himself would be the first to agree, he deserves a chapter to himself.

F

CHAPTER EIGHT

Oswald Bastable

AMONGST ALL the characters authors have invented to tell their stories in the first person, Oswald Bastable holds an honourable place, if for nothing else than for his original approach to his story.

From the moment he introduces himself Oswald is no character in a book, but the most amusing of all the boys the reader knows. He never describes his looks clearly, a hint here and there but no more, yet he is quietly confident, and rightly, that everybody who reads about him would recognise him instantly, should they have the fortune to meet him. He is like the child who, when asked what they were drawing, replied 'God'. 'But you can't draw God, darling,' their mother said, 'nobody knows what He looks like.' 'They will,' the child answered, 'when I've finished.' By the time Oswald lays his pen down at the end of the *New Treasure Seekers*, it would be a dense reader indeed who did not know Oswald as well as they know the members of their own family.

'It was Oswald who first thought of looking for treasure. Oswald often thinks of very interesting things. And directly he thought of it he did not keep it to himself, as some boys would have done, but he told the others.'

Having made this clear statement about the subject of his book and given his readers their first hint of his quality, though of course remaining the anonymous writer, Oswald then gives quickly and clearly the reasons why treasure is needed, and small fragments of news to help the readers to get to know his family. Dora was trying to mend a large hole in one of Noël's stockings: 'Dora is the only one of us who ever tries to mend anything.' What a picture that gives of the Bastables, with their uncared-for look, and incidentally of Dora. In describing Alice's efforts to make things he draws another picture of the family's appearance: 'Most of our things are black or grey since Mother died.' Poor children, it was hard enough for them getting on without their mother, and it cannot have made it easier that they had the constant reminder of being dressed in mourning. And what a picture of a date that description of the blacks and greys gives. The children were still in mourning, because 'Father does not like you to ask for new things'. Yet when Mother died, though Father was ill, that the children, even little H. O., should not be clothed in suitable mourning was unthinkable, as E. Nesbit remembered only too well from the days when she, a small thing of four, was dressed in mourning, quite possibly black with crape on it, for her father.

E. Nesbit, having conceived Oswald, was able to use him to speak for her. Except for Lewis Carroll in his opening of *Alice in Wonderland*: 'And what is the use of a book,' thought Alice, 'without pictures or conversation?', no author has been able to lay down so clearly what in their opinion a children's book should be, as E. Nesbit. 'The best part of books is when things are happening. That is the best part of real things too. This is why I shall not tell you in this story about all the days when nothing happened. You will not catch me saying, "thus the sad days passed slowly by" – or "the years rolled on their weary course" – or "time went on" – because it is silly; of course time goes on – whether you say so or not. So I shall just tell you the nice, interesting parts – and in between you will understand that we had our meals and got up and went to bed, and dull things like that. It would be sickening to write all that down, though of course it happens.'

Lovers of the E. Nesbit books may disagree with her, and wish sometimes less happened, as her families, when pausing before a new adventure, are at their best, but it is interesting to know through Oswald how her mind worked when she was brooding on an idea for one of her books for children.

None of the Bastables are so young for their age as Oswald. He cannot have been less than twelve and could have been thirteen. Even allowing for the fact that children were far younger for their ages when E. Nesbit wrote about the Bastables, Oswald is allowed to be downright childish on occasion. It is impossible to believe, and I am sure E. Nesbit did not, that a boy of twelve or thirteen, let along a girl of perhaps fourteen, could be fooled into thinking they had found the half-crowns which had so palpably come out of Albert-next-door's Uncle's pocket, yet they did, for Oswald records: 'We looked at each other, speechless with surprise and delight, like in books.' The answer is probably in the customs of the time of which she was writing. Small children would not have been allowed to roam about alone, but would have been confined to the garden unless someone adult could go with them. In the long period when the book an author is planning to write is simmering in their mind, no doubt the adventures of the Bastables were thought out in detail by E. Nesbit, and, if she worked

from notes, jotted down. But of course almost none of
the adventures she planned could have taken place had
there been an adult around, so she resorted to a neat
trick, she only gives the ages of the twins and H. O.,
the ages of the others she leaves in the air. If there are
readers so prosaic they must know every detail, let
them work out the ages of Dora, Oswald and Dicky for
themselves, but do not let them hope E. Nesbit is going
to spoil her book for such as they, her children are the
ages she wants them to be for the purposes of her story,
and that should be enough for anyone.

One reason why E. Nesbit does not date is that she
understood the essence of childhood. 'But H. O. did
did not care about waiting, and I felt for him. Dora
is rather like grown-ups in that way; she does not
seem to understand that when you want a thing you
do want it, and that you don't wish to wait, even a
minute.' The cave man's child wanted the promised
carved stone promised by his father then, not next
week. The child today, told he can take his boat to
the pond, is not interested in a vague 'sometime', he
wants to go now. Oswald was always properly indignant of delays. 'Some people have no idea of the value
of time. And Dora is one of those who do not understand that when you want to do a thing you *do* want to,
and not to do something else, and perhaps your own
thing, a week later.' E. Nesbit was one of the fortunate
who remained young in heart, or even her blotting-
paper memory might have failed her, for how things
spoil by being kept is easily forgotten by grown-ups.

E. Nesbit, although she might play about with her
children's ages, never writes down to an imagined age
group. She uses the words that feel to her right, and if
her readers did not know them, then there was
always the dictionary. 'We laughed – because we

knew what an amphora is. If you don't you might look it up in the dicker. It's not a flower, though it sounds like one out of the gardening book, the kind you never hear of anyone growing.' It would have been easy for Oswald to have said what amphorae were, but apart from the fact that E. Nesbit believed in looking things up in the dictionary, it was not the way her mind worked, she wrote about intelligent children for intelligent children, for even when her children were doing something foolish, they remained good thinkers.

Oswald draws a remarkable picture of himself. 'My father is prompt and decisive in action, so is his eldest son.' 'Oswald did not feel quite sure Father would like us to go asking for shillings and sixpences, or even half-crowns, from strangers, but he did not say so. The money had been asked for and got, and it couldn't be helped – and perhaps he wanted the pudding – I am not able to remember exactly why he did not speak up and say, "This is wrong," but anyway he didn't.' 'Oswald (this has more than once happened) was the first to restore his manners. He made a proper bow like he has been taught.' 'Alice was knitting by the fire; it was for Father, but I am sure his feet are not at all that shape. He has a high and beautifully formed instep like Oswald's.' 'Oswald is a very modest boy, I believe, but even he would not deny that he has an active brain. The author has heard both his father and Albert's uncle say so. And the most far-reaching ideas often come to him quite naturally – just as silly notions that aren't any good might come to you.' 'And I was glad I'd owned up, for Father slapped me on the back, and said I was a young brick, and our robber said I was no funk anyway, and though I got very hot under the blanket I liked it, and I explained that the others would have done the same if they had thought of it.' 'But Oswald tries to make allowances even for people who do not wash their ears.'

There is scarcely a page of the Bastable books which has not some gem on it which shows the Oswaldishness of Oswald. Few could argue that he is by far the most original of the children in the Nesbit portrait gallery.

It is interesting to speculate why, having discovered how brilliantly she could tell a story through the mouth of one of her characters, E. Nesbit deserted the idea for direct story telling. Today when even the best children's writers seem to find a formula and stick to it her various ways of telling her story and her complete change in type of story is refreshing. It is of course possible, and indeed it seems likely, that book selling was less commercialised than it is at the present time and so she did not suffer from publishers both at home and in America who asked incessantly for more about the Bastables, or another book about the Psammead, or if she did she paid no attention. She was of course far better placed financially than our present-day writers. She is said to have made £2,000 a year out of her children's books, which would be roughly £6,000 today, and of course by today's standards income tax was very low so she was able to keep most of her earnings. But even so it is interesting the way she was able to abandon her characters at the height of their success and invent a new set, and a new way of telling their story, and to move from the everyday world into fantasy and back again, gathering a new public as she went. It is hard to believe today that either his publishers or his readers would be pleased if Arthur Ransome were to desert his real children and their holiday adventures and produce a magic animal that transported them anywhere they wished. But whatever the reason, either because E. Nesbit flouted the publisher's wishes or because her inventive mind refused to be trammelled by 'I'm afraid we shan't get the sales for this that we had for the last because the public expect more about the Psammead or the Mouldiwarp, or whatever it was –', she told whatever story it was in her mind to tell, and for that reason she is the most exhilarating writer to study.

Except for *The Railway Children*, the Bastables are the most solid family group E. Nesbit gave her public. This is partly due to the fact already mentioned that her children clung to each other because they had no one else to cling to, for their father was absorbed in business and their mother was dead. There is too the feeling of permanence, again already mentioned, by the family words. The children do not begin when the book begins, for they have had a past to which words and jokes belong. H. O., for instance, is not christened in the book. He was named after an advertisement long before the story starts. And in all three books there are casual mentions of events which happened before the readers began to know the children. As an example, quite unexplained there is this charming expression: it is in relation to the booby-trap hamper sent to the porter and the shame when the porter's old father-in-law came to call: 'It was hard. But it was ginger-ale and seed cake compared to having to tell Father. . . .' To what does the ginger-ale and seed cake relate? When had the children had a meal of ginger-ale and seed cake, which had stayed in their memories to such an extent it was an understood family expression? In the *New Treasure Seekers*, without any tiresome footnote saying '*Read*

The Woudlbegoods,' Oswald says he always liked Denny to have ideas of his own, 'because it was us who taught him the folly of white-mousishness'. This is typically E. Nesbit. The Bastables are real, they do not belong to one book or another book. Denny, as E. Nesbit had first known him, did suffer from white-mousishness and it was the Bastables who cured him, and she takes it for granted that her readers know this and if they do not and would wish to, then they can find out about Denny and Daisy for themselves. Certainly she is not going to tell them to read her past books.

Perhaps nothing shows E. Nesbit's gift for writing for children more clearly than the ability she has for making her children live. It is not possible to find out how long she existed with her characters before she put pen to paper. The time this takes varies from author to author, but one thing is certain, she never wrote a word of the Bastables until she knew them better than the children around her, for only by knowing everything about her characters, infinitely more than she had any intention of using, could she have made them live and breathe to such an extent that when Oswald wrote at the end of *The New Treasure Seekers* that this was the last story that the present author was going to write, it did not mean for her readers that the Bastable Saga had come to an end. It was more as if a family of children who lived next door, and were so well known they were like part of the family, had moved to another place where, though you might not see them they were still enjoying their vivid and exciting lives. To be able to do this is a quality possessed by the very few, and so it is no wonder that E. Nesbit's books still live and will live for countless children yet unborn.

CHAPTER NINE

Robert, Anthea, Jane, Cyril and the Lamb

IN STUDYING Robert, Anthea, Jane, Cyril and the Lamb, the five children who appear in E. Nesbit's magic trilogy, *Five Children and It, The Phoenix and the Carpet* and *The Story of the Amulet*, it seems necessary to think of her state of mind when she was first brooding on the Psammead. E. Nesbit, though it brought her little money, was accepted as a poetess and writer of prose and novels in the highest literary circles. But it was not until she wrote her first two books about the Bastables that fortune and wide-scale fame came her way. It is doubtful if any writer who has chosen a career in literature intended for adults is properly appreciative of fame and fortune which comes to them through books for children. Would Robert Louis Stevenson be pleased if he could come back today and find his name very much alive but not for his work for adults, but because of *Treasure Island* and *The Child's Garden of Verses*? What would Rudyard Kipling say if he found that his prose and poems for adults were in eclipse, even if only temporarily, whereas there can be few people who consider themselves even mildly educated who were not brought up on The Jungle Books? It is conceivable, therefore, that Nesbit, though deeply grateful on one hand to the Bastable children, who had enabled her to dismiss the wolf for ever from her doorstep, was on the other hand a little jealous of them. It was hard wherever she went to be recognised not as the author of this book of poems or that book of prose, but as the inventor of the Bastables. 'My children will be so excited I've met you, they simply love your books.' In time she got used to her position as a great figure in the world of children's literature, but at first it must have had its galling side.

It is only if E. Nesbit as an adult writer is seen fighting her successful other half – the writer for children – that the form of the first three magic books becomes understandable. For she who had such ability to bring her children alive, succeeded throughout three books in keeping Robert, Anthea, Jane and Cyril so much in the background that even if they had the Lamb with them nobody could possibly have recognized them if they had sat opposite them in a bus. Grateful though she probably was to her public, she would have got fed up with too much fan mail. It was kind of her readers to write, but too many letters, all on the same subject could be a bore, especially to someone who would rather be congratulated on a book of poems. But it was her fate to be asked for more, and ever more about the Bastables. Presumably to avoid the same thing happening when the first of her magic books came out she played a trick on her readers. Never throughout the three books in which Robert, Anthea, Jane and Cyril appear does she give them a surname. And this is an extraordinary effective means of keeping a family in the background. It is one thing to write a letter saying 'Dear Miss Nesbit, I simply love the Bastables, please write another book about them', and quite another to write 'Dear Miss Nesbit, I simply love Robert, Anthea, Jane, Cyril and the Lamb, please write another book about them.' She did not even, in the first magic book, allow a creature to settle down as a popular figure, for no sooner had the Psammead won its way into thousands of hearts in *Five Children and It* than she dropped it in favour of the Phoenix in *The Phoenix and the Carpet*, and when that most delicious bird became number one favourite she allowed it to remain burnt up for perhaps another two thousand years, and brought back the Psammead, but with its gifts changed, for in *The Story of the Amulet* it will be remembered it was the Amulet who worked the magic, for the Psammead could only grant wishes to outsiders.

There is another point too in E. Nesbit turning from a family story to one mainly to be filled with magic And this is what she wrote herself, or rather caused Oswald to write: 'The best part of books is when things are happening'. In the Bastable books, in the nature of events, there were pauses when only family business went on, but in the magic books it is very seldom indeed that nothing is happening or about to happen, so in writing them she was giving children the sort of story she believed they would, when they got over missing the Bastables, most enjoy.

Although in the Robert, Anthea, Jane and Cyril series E. Nesbit told her story direct, as opposed to in the first person, she still followed a certain pattern. In each book there is, if not a home, then a well-described house which is the children's background. In *Five Children and It* home was one taken for the holidays: 'The White House was on the edge of a hill, with a wood behind it – and the chalk-quarry on one side and the gravel-pit on the other. Down at the bottom of the hill was a level plain, with queer-shaped white buildings where people burnt lime, and a big red brewery and other houses; and when the big chimneys were smoking and the sun was setting, the valley looked as if it was filled with golden mist, and the limekilns and oast-houses glimmered and glittered till they were like an enchanted city out of the *Arabian Nights.*'

In *The Phoenix and the Carpet* the children are living at their real home, at 18, Camden Terrace, Camden Town. There is rather a mixed account of this house: 'So the egg was put on the mantelpiece, where it quite brightened up the dingy nursery. The nursery was dingy, because it was a basement room, and its windows looked out on a stone area with a rockery made of clinkers facing the windows. Nothing grew in the rockery except London pride and snails.

'The room had been described in the house agent's list as a "convenient breakfast-room in basement", and in the daytime it was rather dark. This did not matter so much in the evenings when the gas was alight, but then it was in the evening the blackbeetles got so sociable, and used to come out of the low cupboards on each side of the fireplace where their homes were, and try to make friends with the children.' In another place the home sounds charming. 'Sunday at 18, Camden Terrace, Camden Town, was always a very pretty day. Father always brought home flowers on Saturday, so that the breakfast-table was extra beautiful. In November, of course, the flowers were chrysanthemums, yellow and coppery coloured. Then there were always sausages on toast for breakfast, and these are rapture, after six days of Kentish Town Road eggs at fourteen a shilling.' In *The Story of the Amulet* the home is Old Nurse's lodgings, already described, in Fitzroy Street near the British Museum. These lodgings could not and were not intended to feel like a home, but, as already shown by quotations from the story, the rooms were most minutely described, so that the reader could see the background to the book.

E. Nesbit also kept to her pattern in that she disposes with great adroitness of the parents. In *Five Children and It*, though the parents are sometimes about, 'Father had to go away suddenly on business, and Mother had gone away to stay with Granny, who was not very well'. And on no occasion were the parents anywhere near the house when they were not wanted. In *The Phoenix and the Carpet* the parents do live in the house, but have so many engagements outside that their author has no difficulty at all in getting rid of them every time the children and the Phoenix are going on a trip by carpet. In *The Story of the Amulet*, which was published three years after *The Phoenix and the Carpet*, E. Nesbit had clearly decided that she had had enough of planning to get the parents out of the way, for in this book she is far more drastic. 'Father had to go out to Manchuria to telegraph news about the war to the tiresome paper he wrote for – The Daily Bellower, or something like that, was its name. And Mother, poor dear Mother, was away in Madeira, because she had been very ill.' Poor dear Mother indeed, E. Nesbit must have smiled as she wrote that, and given an amused nod to father, packed off to Manchuria. 'In this book,' she probably said to herself, 'I won't even have one parent around. How blissful not to have to think about them.' In *The Story of the Amulet* E. Nesbit got rid of the Lamb too, and no wonder, for a baby, even the best of babies, is a great nuisance to its author, when it is intended their family shall constantly disappear into the past through an amulet arch. So the Lamb was packed off to Madeira with Mother. As well, to make it quite obvious that the children had to live in lodgings near the British Museum with Old Nurse, because they had nowhere else to go, E. Nesbit also got rid of the relations. 'Aunt Emma, who was Mother's sister, had suddenly married Uncle Reginald, who was Father's brother, and they had gone to China, which is much too far off for you to expect to be asked to spend the holidays in, however fond your aunt and uncle may be of you.' A delightfully Nesbit touch; no writer was ever more nimble at arriving at the setting they wanted by getting rid of extraneous characters.

What were Robert, Anthea, Jane and Cyril like? They were united in many things, but most noticeably in their love for their baby brother. It is not all children who would wish to have a baby brother constantly with them, but on almost every occasion these children did. And when their author had sent the child to Madeira, they endlessly lamented his absence. They had too, firm codes of family behaviour. 'For the worst of it was that these four children, with a very proper dislike of anything even faintly bordering on the sneakish, had a law, unalterable as those of the Medes and Persians, that one had to stand by the results of a toss-up, or a drawing of lots, or any other appeal to chance, however much one might happen to dislike the way things were turning out.' 'You know, of course, that it is stealing to take a new stick of chalk, but it is not wrong to take a broken piece, so long as you only take one.' 'Yet no one would have dared to suggest that the charm should not be used; and though each was in its heart very frightened indeed, they would all have joined in jeering at the cowardice of any one of them who should have uttered the timid but natural suggestion, "Don't let's!"'

There were also family beliefs, as for instance the way to ensure that you woke up at a certain time. 'You get into bed at night, and lie down quite flat on your little back, with your hands straight down by your sides. Then you say "I *must* wake up at five" (or six, or seven, or eight, or nine, or whatever the time is that you want), and as you say it you push your chin down on to your chest and then bang your head back on the pillow. And you do this as many times as there are ones in the time you want to wake up at. (It is quite an easy sum). Of course everything depends on your really wanting to get up at five (or six, or seven, or eight, or nine); if you don't really want to, it's all of no use. But if you do – well, try it and see. Of course in this, as in doing Latin proses or getting into mischief, practice makes perfect.'

The question of what is right in the eyes of the family crops up here and there. 'We'll club our money, though, and leave it to pay for the things, won't we?' Anthea was persuasive, and very nearly in tears, because it is most trying to feel enormously hungry and unspeakably sinful at one and the same time.

One of the difficulties in getting to know the children, as apart from the magic animals, in the first three magic books, is E. Nesbit's deliberate vagueness about the family's finances. In *Five Children and It* the house taken for the summer was clearly not the sort of house that well-to-do people would take. It was a house deep in the country with no other house in sight, 'and the children had been in London for two years, without so much as once going to the seaside

'*Poof, poof, poofy,*' *he said, and made a grab*

FIVE CHILDREN AND IT

But there's only half of it there!

THE STORY OF THE AMULET

even for a day by an excursion train'. And when they arrived 'Mother, curiously enough, was in no hurry to get out'; which was understandable for 'it was not really a pretty house at all; it was quite ordinary, and mother thought it was rather inconvenient, and was quite annoyed at there being no shelves, to speak of, and hardly a cupboard in the place'. Yet in *The Phoenix and the Carpet* there are several servants, including a nurse-maid called Martha, and every suggestion that money is no object, as when father sent the telegram about the theatre. 'Box for kiddies at Garrick. Stalls for us, Haymarket. Meet Charing Cross, 6.30.' But in *The Story of the Amulet*, admitting that it had taken a lot of money to send Mother and the Lamb to Madeira, the children were not only parked in rather dreary lodgings, but with very little pocket money, so that they were reduced, they supposed, to spending their holiday seeing things in London which they did not have to pay to see. Then again in *The Phoenix and the Carpet* the children appear to be exceptionally well-dressed. 'The streets there were small and stuffy and ugly, and crowded with printers' boys and binders' girls coming out from work; and these stared so hard at the pretty red coats and caps of the sisters that they wished they had gone some other way. And the printers and binders made very personal remarks, advising Jane to get her hair cut, and inquiring where Anthea had bought that hat.' The occasion was the famous one in which the Phoenix visited the headquarters of its very own fire office. The scene described took place between Fetter Lane and Ludgate Circus, so the children must have been noticeably well turned out to attract such attention there. And indeed the boys said: 'It's partly you girls' fault, coming out in those flashy coats.' And on

G

the occasion of the box at the Garrick the whole family seem to have been splendidly dressed. In the restaurant before the theatre Robert, who it will be remembered, had the Phoenix buttoned inside his coat – 'had to pretend to be cold at the glittering, many-mirrored restaurant where they all had dinner, with father in evening dress, with a very shiny white shirt-front, and mother looking lovely in her grey evening dress, that changes into pink and green when she moves.' But although the children's ordinary lives and everyday existence is kept to the background of the three books, it is remarkable that they live as clearly as they do in the gloriously magical world to which their author transplanted them.

E. Nesbit's powers as a magician grow from book to book, until in *The Story of the Amulet* nothing is impossible, and nothing that she writes is unbelievable. In creating those so different but equally brilliant creatures, the Psammead and the Phoenix, she was opening the door of the everyday world, and leading her readers out of their nurseries and schoolrooms into the vast world which lies as far as the imagination can stretch. And from the very beginning she warned her readers she was going to do this. 'I feel that I could go on and make this into a most interesting story about all the ordinary things that the children did, – just the kind of things you do yourself, you know,– and you would believe every word of it; and when I told about the children's being tiresome, as you are sometimes, your aunts would perhaps write in the margin of the story with a pencil, "How true!" or "How like life!" and you would see it and very likely be annoyed. So I will only tell you the really astonishing things that happened. . . .'

And when the astonishing things did happen, what

scope it gave her imagination. 'Of course you all know what flying feels like, because everyone has dreamed about flying, and it seems so beautifully easy – only, you can never remember how you did it; and as a rule you have to do it without wings, in your dreams, which is more clever and uncommon, but not so easy to remember the rule for . . .' Although in *Five Children and It* E. Nesbit had not got the hold on magic that she was to have by the time she reached *The Story of the Amulet,* she was already beginning to make it possible to live in two dimensions at the same time. '"Yes, but look here, Squirrel," said Robert; "you're so clever at explaining about invisibleness and all that. How is it the biscuits are here, and all the bread and meat and things have disappeared?"' '"I don't know," said Cyril after a pause, "unless it's because *we* had them. Nothing about us has changed. Everything's in my pocket all right."' '"Then if we *had* the mutton it would be real," said Robert. "Oh, don't I wish we could find it!"' '"But we can't find it. I suppose it isn't ours till we've got it in our mouths."' And so it goes on, E. Nesbit working out the problem for the children, of how food that belongs to one dimension can reach your stomach in another. Or in *The Story of the Amulet.* 'Time is only a mode of thought, you know.' The children thrilled to the familiar words: 'So you know that too, do you?' said Cyril. 'It is part of the mystery of all magic, is it not?' said the priest. That time is part of the mystery of all magic was a big truth for Nesbit to give her children readers. But the more she wrote about magic the more sure she was that magic was not something invented, but something that existed, and was there for everybody who was capable of believing in it. How many children, because of the Nesbit books, must have dug in sand pits for Psammeads, and searched for golden eggs which, when put on a fire, would hatch out a phoenix? Or have turned up the corners of every carpet in the house hoping that this might be the magic one, perhaps a few even accepted that time is not then nor now, but always.

Because they belong to the first three magic books, it should be possible to write here about those two fabulous creatures, the Psammead and the Phoenix. But even the slightest study of the E. Nesbit books, and it is clear it would be the gravest mistake to allow these two to meet on paper. The Psammead had its moments of gentleness, but it was as a rule tough and outspoken, and not mindful of the feelings of others. The Phoenix, on the other hand, as might be expected, was a mannered bird accustomed to exquisite behaviour and expecting it in return. It seems therefore best to give each a chapter to itself, starting, if the Phoenix will excuse the liberty, with the Psammead.

CHAPTER TEN

The Psammead

ALTHOUGH SHE was never fond of describing the looks of human beings E. Nesbit was very clear what her fabulous creatures looked like. The Psammead, when it was first seen, coming out of the sand, yawning and rubbing the ends of its eyes with its hands, was a surprising beast to meet. 'It's eyes were on long horns like a snail's eyes, and it could move them in and out like telescopes; it had ears like a bat's ears, and its tubby body was shaped like a spider's and covered with thick soft fur; its legs and arms were furry too, and it had hands and feet like a monkey's.' It is clear that E. Nesbit did not write about the Psammead until she had known it intimately in her mind for a long time. The Psammead, like the Bastables, is a creation about which the author knew far more than she put down in her books. She had not only a smattering of knowledge about its career covering the several thousand years before she introduced it in *Five Children and It,* but also about its future in the Past, when *The Story of the Amulet* ends. But even knowing it so well herself, could she have guessed that in spite of the very unattractive picture she drew of its appearance, that the Psammead would find its way into millions of hearts?

Appearance apart, the Psammead was not an easy creature to know: 'It isn't talking I mind, – as long as you're reasonably civil. But I'm not going to make polite conversation for you. If you talk nicely to me, perhaps I'll answer you, and perhaps I won't. Now say something.' It had occasionally, as for instance when it was alone with Anthea, its softer moments. '"Thank you, – you really are rather thoughtful." It crept on to her lap and snuggled down, and she put her arms round it with a rather frightened gentleness. "Now then!" It said.

'"Well then," said Anthea, "everything that we've wished has turned out rather horrid. I wish you would advise us. You are so old, you must be very wise."

'"I was always generous from a child,– I've spent the whole of my waking hours in giving. But one thing I won't give – that's advice."'

The creature – and no wonder – seeing how long it had been around, was educated. When Anthea asked why their wishes had not just vanished, the Psammead replied: '*Autres temps, autres moeurs.*' But it was also a master of what in military circles is known as dumb insolence. 'It almost snarled as it shook its whiskers, and turned a sulky brown back on them. The most hopeful felt that further parley was vain.'

No creature ever invented has kept its end up better against what, on the surface appeared to be hopeless odds. Dumb insolence and terse words apart, the children, if they had cared to think about it in that way, had the Psammead in their power. It had to grant their wishes whether it liked it or not. It was brilliant writing that made the Psammead somehow keep its dignity, make the granting of a wish a favour, and force the reader to worry about its personal comforts. Water, even one drop of rain, was, it will be remembered, anathema to it, and its only form of sustenance was sand, as was to be expected of a sand fairy.

Somehow, in the thousands of years of its existence, it had learnt how to handle human beings, to make them feel they were being a nuisance. 'You want another wish, I expect. But I can't keep on slaving from morning till night giving people their wishes. I must have *some* time to myself.' 'I'd almost burst myself to give you one wish after another, as long as I held out, if you'd only never, never ask me to do it after today. If you knew how I hate to blow myself out with other people's wishes, and how frightened I am always that I shall strain a muscle or something. And then to wake up every morning and know you've *got* to do it. You don't know what it is. . . .'

It is no wonder the Psammead's dry husky voice rings in the reader's ears long after the books are put away, nor that it stays in the mind when the characters from other books, even august books, are forgotten. It is such a permanent sort of creature, after all it was granting wishes, angrily and unwillingly, in the good old Megatherium days. 'For a creature that had in its time associated with Megatheriums and Pterodactyls, its quickness was really wonderful.' Obviously, though a thousand years or so may pass before the Psammead is disturbed again, there can be no doubt in the minds of those who know it that it will be granting wishes, when the right time comes, to another family of fortunate children.

But what was E. Nesbit planning for the Psammead when she wrote the end of *Five Children and It*?

'"Thank you kindly for all you've done for us, and I hope you'll have a good long sleep, and I hope we shall see you again some day."'

'"Is that a wish?" it said in a weak voice.'

'"Yes, please," said the two girls together.'

'Then for the last time in this story they saw the

Psammead blow itself out and collapse suddenly. It nodded to them, blinked its long snail's eyes, burrowed, and disappeared, scratching fiercely to the last, and the sand closed over it.'

So it had to come back, it was a promise to E. Nesbit's public, just as clearly as it was a promise made to Anthea and Jane. Its author presumably picked it up, and laid it, cosily, in sand it is to be hoped, in the lumber room of her mind, where it could rest until she was ready to bring it into another book.

Nothing shows E. Nesbit's ability to use her creations to suit her own ends more clearly than the manner of the Psammead's return. She had at the time when he was due to reappear made a friend who was profoundly to influence her writing, and therefore to influence the behaviour and utterances of the Psammead. He was Doctor Wallis, afterwards Sir Wallis, Budge, Keeper of Egyptian and Assyrian Antiquities at the British Museum. This was the man who taught her what could be expected of an Amulet, about Words of Power, and either put into her head, or caused her to think more deeply, on the relativity of time. As well it was he who, drawing from the well of his knowledge, was able to show her Babylon and ancient Egypt.

Now where was the Psammead to fit in? That rugged little individualist could not take second place to an Amulet, yet an Amulet there had to be, for the search for the second half and the pin was the *raison d'être* for the adventures planned by E. Nesbit and Dr. Budge. At what period in planning the book did she take a look at the sleeping Psammead in the lumber room of her mind, and recall some of its utterances in its dry husky voice, and conceive one of her most brilliant ideas? The creature had always been intelligent; it could, because she had made it so in *Five Children and It*, no longer grant wishes to the family, why then should it not on its reappearance become a counsellor, guide, and in so far as its nature allowed, a friend? In this capacity it could keep all its old attributes, its moods, its dumb insolence, its brusqueness amounting to rudeness, but it could, with assistance from another character, be the mouthpiece for Doctor Wallis Budge.

So when the Psammead reappears in *The Story of the Amulet* it almost at once begins to play its new part. It was brilliant of E. Nesbit, in spite of her plans for it, to allow the Psammead from its first appearance to be so entirely itself. Its circumstances at the time, it will be remembered, were unfortunate, but nothing could bend that proud neck, or whatever the equivalent to a neck there might be between the eyes on horns and the bat's ears, and the tubby spider-shaped body. It was for sale as a 'mangy old monkey' in a pet shop which sold 'goldfish and white mice, and sea-anemones and other aquarium beasts, and lizards and toads, and hedgehogs and tortoises, and tame rabbits and guinea-pigs. . . .' The Psammead was looking shocking. 'It seemed much thinner than when he had last seen it. It was dusty and dirty, and its fur was untidy and ragged. It had hunched itself up into a miserable lump, and its long snail's eyes were drawn in quite tight so that they hardly showed at all.' But it kept its dignity, and had an excuse ready to account for its appearance. 'I don't think the creature who keeps this shop will ask a very high price for me. I've bitten him more than once, and I've made myself look as common as I can. He's never had a glance from my beautiful, beautiful eyes.'

It was the next day after a nice rest in some silver

sand, brought from the oil and colour shop, that the
Psammead started out on its changed career.

'"Look here," it said; "you must have some new
kind of charm."' And then in the most casual way it
produced the necessary information that led to the
children's half of the Amulet. But even when instruct-
ing the children as to what they should do with their
half, the Psammead was endearingly the old sand
fairy of *Five Children and It*. 'You are not particularly nice, nor particularly clever, and you're not at
all good-looking. Still, you've saved my life – oh,
when I think of that man and his pail of water! – so
I'll tell you all I know. At least, of course I can't do
that, because I know far too much. But I'll tell you
all I know about this red thing.' And when after, for
it, a rather flowery description of the power of the
whole Amulet, it stated that it could also give you
your heart's desire, there follows this typically Psammead conversation:

'"Now you're talking," said Robert.
'"Of course I am," retorted the Psammead tartly,
"so there's no need for you to."'

It was not the Psammead who first spoke of Words
of Power, but it knew all about them and their importance.

'"I've no patience with you . . . if you can't read
you must find someone who can. A priest now?"

'"We don't know any priests," said Anthea; "we
know a clergyman – he's called a priest in the prayer-
book, you know – but he only knows Greek and
Latin and Hebrew, and this isn't either of those –
I know."

'The Psammead stamped a furry foot angrily.

'"I wish I'd never seen you," it said; "You aren't

any more good than so many stone images. Not so much, if I'm to tell the truth. Is there no wise man in your Babylon who can pronounce the names of the Great Ones?"

'"There's a poor learned gentleman upstairs," said Anthea, "we might try him. He has a lot of stone images in his room, and iron-looking ones too – we peeped in once when he was out. Old Nurse says he doesn't eat enough to keep a canary alive. He spends it all on stones and things."

'"Try him," said the Psammead, "only be careful. If he knows a greater name than this and uses it against you, your charm will be of no use. Bind him first with the chains of honour and upright dealing. And then ask his aid."'

When the half Amulet was speaking in its small beautiful voice, the Psammead in its new position was sitting by to interpret.

'"The part of the Amulet which is lost," said the beautiful voice, "was broken and ground into the dust of the shrine that held it. It and the pin that joined the two halves are themselves dust, and the dust is scattered over many lands and sunk in many seas."

'"Oh, I say!" murmured Robert, and a blank silence fell.

'"Then it's all up?" said Cyril at last; "it's no use our looking for a thing that's smashed into dust, and the dust scattered all over the place."

'"If you would find it," said the voice, "you must seek it where it still is, perfect as ever."

'"I don't understand," said Cyril.

'"In the Past you may find it," said the voice.

'"I wish we *may* find it," said Cyril.

'The Psammead whispered crossly, "Don't you understand? The thing existed in the Past. If you were in the Past, too, you could find it. It's very difficult to make you understand things. Time and space are only forms of thought."

'"I see," said Cyril.

'"No, you don't," said the Psammead, "and it doesn't matter if you don't, either. What I mean is that if you were only made the right way, you could see everything happening in the same place at the same time. Now do you see?"

'"I'm afraid *I* don't," said Anthea; "I'm sorry I'm so stupid."

'"Well, at any rate you see this. That lost half of the Amulet is in the Past. Therefore it's in the Past we must look for it. I mustn't speak to the charm myself. Ask it things! Find out!"'

The Psammead would have had less chance to be itself if E. Nesbit had not invented the poor learned gentleman upstairs. This invaluable character was at a guess what she believed Doctor Wallis Budge must have been like at the beginning of his career. If this were not so, there is no understanding why Rekhmarā and the poor learned gentleman became one, and as one person were given the complete Amulet that the children saw in the British Museum of the future. Doctor Wallis Budge's knowledge of ancient Egypt and Assyria was so deep as perhaps to E. Nesbit to seem to need explaining, so she fused him with Rekh-marā, a divine father of the Temple of Amen Rā, who belonged to ancient Egypt before the days of Pharaoh, and that obviously could account for brilliance past her understanding. She also, it is to be supposed, perhaps because she hated to be thought ever to be rude to him, drew Doctor Budge as the nicest of the British Museum staff.

'"But we don't wish to use harsh measures," added the nice one, who was really very nice indeed, and seemed to be over all the others.'

It must have hurt E. Nesbit to say good-bye to the Psammead. All writers create characters of which they grow so fond that they cannot see their pens, or the keys of their typewriters, for the tears in their eyes when the time comes to say good-bye. Perhaps that is why the Psammead, in many ways the most lovable of Nesbit's magic creatures, is allowed to disappear so quietly.

'"And what's to become of *me*? I shall be found out, and made a show of, and degraded in every possible way. I *know* they'll make me go into Parliament – hateful place – all mud and no sand. That beautiful Baalbec temple in the desert! Plenty of good sand there, and no politics! I wish I were there, safe in the Past – that I do."

'"I wish you were," said the learned gentleman absently, yet polite as ever.

'The Psammead swelled itself up, turned its long snail's eyes in one last lingering look at Anthea – a loving look, she always said, and thought – and – vanished.'

And vanish it did, for E. Nesbit never wrote about it again.

CHAPTER ELEVEN

The Phoenix

WHEN E. NESBIT brought the Phoenix to London the manner of its arrival was delightful. Its golden egg, it will be remembered, arrived rolled up in a magic carpet. To get at one and the same time a magic carpet and a phoenix egg is strawberries and cream on top of birthday cake. To enhance her readers' pleasure E. Nesbit, who was always good at dotting her 'i's', made the man who had sold the carpet, not only refuse to hear he had included a phoenix egg, but drive the children from his shop.

'"Clear out, I say!" he shouted, "or I'll call for the police. A nice thing for customers to 'ear you acoming 'ere a-charging me with finding things in goods what I sells. 'Ere, be off, afore I sends you off with a flea in your ears. Hi! constable. . . ."'

A most satisfactory beginning to a book in which the Phoenix hatched from that egg was to play such a part, for Anthea, Robert, Jane and Cyril, like all Nesbit's children, preferred when circumstances permitted to be on the side of the angels. The hatching of the egg came about because the children were playing at magic, so the setting for its re-birth was all the Phoenix could expect of an English nursery.

'"I'm sure a magic fire ought to be made of sweet-smelling wood, and have magic gums and essences and things in it."

'"I don't know any sweet-smelling wood, except cedar," said Robert; "but I've got some ends of cedar-wood lead pencil."

'So they burned the ends of lead pencil. And still nothing happened.

'"Let's burn some of the eucalyptus oil we have for our colds," said Anthea.

'And they did. It certainly smelt very strong. And they burned lumps of camphor out of the big chest. It was very bright, and made a horrid black smoke, which looked very magical. But still nothing happened. Then they got some clean tea-cloths from the dresser drawer in the kitchen, and waved them over the magic chalk-tracings, and sang "The Hymn of the Moravian Nuns at Bethlehem", which is very impressive. And still nothing happened. So they waved more and more wildly, and Robert's tea-cloth caught the golden egg and whisked it off the mantelpiece, and it fell into the fender and rolled under the grate.'

The bird when it hatched out was exquisite to look at, and though self-willed had perfect manners. It, or rather its egg, had been lying in the lumber room of E. Nesbit's mind for a long while, so she knew it intimately from the moment it 'rose in its nest of fire, stretched its wings, and flew out into the room,' saying as it perched on the fender: '"Be careful; I am not nearly cool yet."' And later, when it had fluttered on to the table, and a faint smell of burning came from the cloth: '"It's only a very little scorched," said the Phoenix, apologetically; "it will come out in the wash."' Not a bad feat of remembering human behaviour for a bird who had last hatched out two thousand years before.

Why did E. Nesbit in this book use someone else's creation, rather than a brand new creature from her own fertile brain? For the Phoenix is mentioned in encyclopaedias as Cyril read out to it, as 'a fabulous bird of antiquity', and once anyone gets trapped in an encyclopaedia it is less easy to do as you like with them. Apart from the fact that Laurence Housman suggested that some time the bird would do well in a book, the probable reason for her using it is that for the time being she had had enough of the Psammead; she had promised his return, and that must content her readers, but while planning where she would take the children with the Psammead's wishes, she had unearthed several glorious ideas that she wanted to use, but for which she needed a creature with a totally different personality from the Psammead's. As well, she had thought up a chapter of such originality that she simply had to use it. This was of course the Phoenix' visit as head of its house, to The Phoenix Fire Office.

Though Housman had suggested using the bird, when she did write about the Phoenix E. Nesbit made the creature entirely her own. True, she stuck to its known history and its date, but after that she did what she pleased with it, and what a personality she gave it. All the creatures in her magic books have to be self-assertive, how otherwise could they hold their positions as the leading character against human children? It was of course born with the advantage that it was exquisite to look at, something even its greatest admirer could not say about the Psammead. Outstanding beauty, when it belongs to those who can think, gives them an air, it sets them apart. The Phoenix had that air. It was of course as completely

'Try another verse,' said the Phoenix

THE PHOENIX AND THE CARPET

Everyone helped – even the Phoenix

THE PHOENIX AND THE CARPET

aware of its looks as have been, and are today, great human beauties.

'"And you won't vanish, or anything sudden will you?" asked Anthea, anxiously.

'"Why?" it asked, puffing out the golden feathers, "do you wish me to stay here?"

'"Oh *yes*," said every one, with unmistakable sincerity.

'"Why?" asked the Phoenix again, looking modestly at the table-cloth.

'"Because," said everyone at once, and then stopped short; only Jane added after a pause, "you are the most beautiful person we've ever seen."'

In the thousands of years of its existence the bird had acquired an immense smattering of knowledge, but it was at no time so profound in its thinking as the Psammead, nor had it troubled to educate itself so well, but it was, as it said itself, 'a singularly observant bird". And like all magic creatures, had no trouble with languages. On each of its re-births it could, had it wished, have got through existence very well on its looks alone, but, like many another proud beauty, it liked to shine with its tongue too, and could become very temperamental when much talking was called for, and it was not prepared:

'"I must have an hour or two's quiet," it said, "I really must. My nerves will give way unless I can get a little rest. You must remember it's two thousand years since I had any conversation – I'm out of practice, and I must take care of myself. I've often been told that mine is a valuable life."'

It was lucky for E. Nesbit's readers that the Phoenix did not wish to go down to posterity as a

H

dumb blonde, for it said many good things. '"These wishing creatures always know all about each other – they're so clannish; like the Scots, you know – all related."

'"Excuse me," said the Phoenix' soft voice breaking in on the general sigh of relief, "but I think these brown people want your cook."

'"To – to eat?" whispered Jane.

'"Hardly," rejoined the bird. "Who wants cooks to *eat*? Cooks are *engaged*, not eaten."'

Although it proved to be an awkward guest to have around, the Phoenix was at times the kindest-hearted, and most adaptable of all the Nesbit creatures; apart from its dislike of water, could anyone imagine the Psammead washing up? But on one occasion the Phoenix did.

'"I should wash up – I mean wash down," the Phoenix said.

'So they did. There was plenty of hot water left in the kettle, and everyone helped – even the Phoenix, who took up cups by their handles with its clever claws and dipped them in the hot water, and then stood them on the table ready for Anthea to dry them.'

But, oh dear, when it allowed adulation to go to its head how difficult the Phoenix could be. Who can forget it in the theatre watching *The Water Babies*?

'What I must tell you is that, though Cyril and Jane and Robert and Anthea enjoyed it as much as any children possibly could, the pleasure of the Phoenix was far, far greater than theirs.

'"This is indeed my temple," it said again and again. "What radiant rites! And all to do honour to me!"'

Later, distressed because there was no altar, no fire, and no incense, it 'became so excited and fretful and tiresome that four at least of the party of five wished deeply that it had been left at home'. 'And then, before any of the children could even begin to think of stopping it, it spread its bright wings and swept round the theatre, brushing its gleaming feathers against delicate hangings and gilded woodwork.' Which ended of course in the theatre burning.

The difficulty was to get rid of the Phoenix, for, unlike the Psammead who always longed to be allowed 'to go to sand', the bird, though it liked its rest, seemed to be enjoying itself in its over-excited way. But at last it decided to go, and a good thing too, for no one could have persuaded it to go against its will. So one day it fluttered up to its favourite perch on the chair-back, and cried:

'". . . oh youthful children of men, restrain your tears of misery and despair, for what must be must be, and I would not remember you, thousands of years hence, as base ingrates and crawling worms compact of low selfishness."

'"I should hope not, indeed," said Cyril.

'"Weep not," the bird went on; "I really do beg that you won't weep. I will not seek to break the news to you gently. Let the blow fall at once. The time has come when I must leave you."'

The children gave the bird what Robert described as 'a jolly good send-off'.

'At the grocer's they bought all the spices they could remember the names of – shell-like mace, cloves like blunt nails, peppercorns, the long and the round kind; ginger, the dry sort, of course; and beautiful bloom-covered shells of fragrant cinnamon. Allspice too, and caraway seeds (caraway seeds that smelt most deadly when the time came for burning them).

'Camphor and oil of lavender were bought at the chemist's, and also a little scent sachet labelled "Violettes de Parme".'

Then, when everything was on the fire, and tears had been shed and good-byes said:

'The bright bird fluttered seven times round the room and settled in the hot heart of the fire. The sweet gums and spices and woods flared and flickered around it, but its golden feathers did not burn. It seemed to grow red-hot to the very inside heart of it – and then before the eight eyes of its friends it fell together, a heap of white ashes, and the flames of the cedar pencils and the sandal-wood box met and joined above it.'

The Phoenix was a character who excited, and occasionally perhaps ran away with, its author. For *The Phoenix and the Carpet* has more queer, difficult to explain to anyone adventures than the other two of her first magic books. To E. Nesbit all things were possible, and she knew you could mix a Phoenix and a magic carpet with a bazaar, or transport first a cook, and then a burglar to a tropical island, and no stupid everyday explanations were needed. But who can doubt it was the Phoenix who encouraged her. And who could doubt that though it had got a little out of hand, that she was sorry to let it out of her life, for its departure would mean:

'. . . everything had suddenly settled down from the rosy wild beauty of magic happenings to the common damp brownness of ordinary November life. . . .'

CHAPTER TWELVE

'The Railway Children'

IN THE same year that she published *The Story of the Amulet*, which said good-bye not only to the Psammead but to Anthea, Robert, Jane and Cyril, E. Nesbit published *The Railway Children*.

What made her write *The Railway Children*? Was it because she felt the need to get back to a family who found their excitements through ordinary everyday adventures, and not through magic? It could have been, for two years before she had published the *New Treasure Seekers*, which, except for a few short stories, officially said good-bye to the Bastables, so she may have missed them. It was a moment, rare for her, when she was freed from all clutching characters, for though undoubtedly she still received piles of mail from children asking for the return of this creature or that person, she knew they could not return. Oswald had written his last book, the Psammead was curled up in sand in the Past, and the Phoenix' egg would not hatch out again for at least two thousand years. So it was the perfect moment to bring to birth a new family.

There can be no question but that Nesbit had known her Railway Children for a very long time indeed, in fact she had probably begun to know them in the early days of her marriage to Hubert Bland. For *The Railway Children* belongs to that period of her life, and has not, as her other children's books have, most of their roots in her childhood. She had, as already stated, had a very hard time as a young wife, when she was left almost penniless by her husband's defaulting partner, and had babies plus the convalescent Hubert to support. The hard years, from first-hand accounts, do not appear to have left an outward mark, for by the time she was successful she could be the gayest and the youngest of heart, of any woman of her age her contemporaries knew. But she was, as her articles about herself show, a child who felt deeply, and Wordsworth wrote a truism when he said that 'The Child is father of the Man', so, because she managed to throw cares aside, there is no reason to suppose she forgot them. Rather, like most writers past or present, she thought 'Some day I'll write about that, and get it out of my system'. It is likely she originally intended to tell her story in an adult novel, for there are signs of this in the character of the mother and in some of the descriptive passages; moreover this is the only book where E. Nesbit went right away from her own blue print for a children's book. It is true she starts, as always, with a home, Edgecombe Villa, where the family lived in their affluent days, but when she reaches Three Chimneys, to which they moved when they were poor, the house is barely described at all, the reason being of course that in this one book home is not a matter of bricks and mortar, but is where Mother is, for Mother in *The Railway Children* is the pivot round which her family revolve, in every sense of the word, for she supports them with her writing, as many years before young Mrs. Hubert Bland had supported hers.

The real story, an invalid husband constantly needing attention, had probably been distracting for the breadwinner at the time, and would certainly have been a nuisance to his author, so Father in *The Railway Children* is packed off to prison for a crime he did not commit. But as the book gained its hold on E. Nesbit, bringing out memories from the lumber room of her mind that she had no idea were lying there, she must have had the feeling that there ought to be an invalid around, so since she could not allow Father out of prison until the last chapter, she brought two to the house. The first was a refugee from Russia, and the second the boy in the red jersey who was left in the railway tunnel when playing Hare and Hounds, and you can almost hear E. Nesbit's 'That's more like it' as the doctor visits, and the patient is either strong enough to sit in the garden, or, in the case of the boy, is being nursed in bed.

The Railway Children stands quite by itself amongst E. Nesbit's books for her drawing of the children, Roberta or Bobbie, Peter and Phyllis. The Bastables, because they were described as Oswald saw them, though a living breathing family, were on occasion larger than life, and the children in the magic books, because they had to be less important than a creature, smaller than life, but the Railway Children are real, so real that not only would they be recognizable sitting opposite their readers in a bus, but could earn that finest tribute a child can pay a character or characters in a book: 'That was a very Railway Children thing to do.'

No writer has ever wasted less time getting her stories started than E. Nesbit. Her opening paragraph perfectly describes the life of children of well-to-do parents living in suburbia.

'They were not railway children to begin with. I

don't suppose they had ever thought about railways except as a means of getting to Maskelyne and Cook's, the Pantomime, Zoological Gardens, and Madame Tussaud's. They were just ordinary suburban children, and they lived with their Father and Mother in an ordinary red-brick-fronted villa, with coloured glass in the front door, a tiled passage that was called a hall, a bath-room with hot and cold water, electric bells, french window, and a good deal of white paint, and "every modern convenience", as the house-agents say.' And later on:

'These three lucky children always had everything they needed: pretty clothes, good fires, a lovely nursery with heaps of toys, and a Mother Goose wall-paper. They had a kind and merry nursemaid, and a dog who was called James, and who was their very own. They also had a Father who was just perfect – never cross, never unjust, and always ready for a game – at least, if at any time he was *not* ready, he always had an excellent reason for it, and explained the reason to the children so interestingly and funnily that they felt sure he couldn't help himself.

'You will think that they ought to have been very happy. And so they were, but they did not know *how* happy till the pretty life in Edgecombe Villa was over and done with, and they had to live a very different life indeed.'

This set the stage quickly and neatly for what was to follow: the men who came to take Father away, the sale of all that was pretty and the retaining of only that which was necessary, the dismissing one by one of the servants, and for the children, especially for Roberta, the knowledge that something was terribly wrong without their knowing what. When the story was coming to life in her mind, E. Nesbit probably conceived each member of the family as playing an equal part in her story, but gradually, as she wrote the book, and she states this clearly, Roberta ran away with her heart and so with her pen.

'I hope you don't mind my telling you a good deal about Roberta. The fact is I am growing very fond of her. The more I observe her the more I love her. And I notice all sorts of things about her that I like.

'For instance, she was quite oddly anxious to make other people happy. And she could keep a secret, a tolerably rare accomplishment. Also she had the power of silent sympathy. That sounds rather dull, I know, but it's not so dull as it sounds. It just means that a person is able to know that you are unhappy, and to love you extra on that account, without bothering you by telling you all the time how sorry she is for you. That was what Bobbie was like. She knew that Mother was unhappy – and that Mother had not told her the reason. So she just loved Mother more and never said a single word that could let Mother know how earnestly her little girl wondered what Mother was unhappy about. This needs practice. It is not so easy as you might think.

'Whatever happened – and all sorts of nice, pleasant ordinary things happened – such as picnics, games, and buns for tea, Bobbie always had these thoughts at the back of her mind. "Mother's unhappy. Why? I don't know. She doesn't want me to know. I won't try to find out. But she is unhappy. Why? I don't know. She doesn't . . ." and so on, repeating and repeating like a tune that you don't know the stopping part of.'

From the first page, because she knew her family

so well before she started to write their story, and because she knew so much both before the story began and after it finished that she was keeping to herself, E. Nesbit knew that she was going to allow Roberta to run away with her.

'Mothers never have favourites, but if their Mother *had* had a favourite, it might have been Roberta.'

But looking at E. Nesbit's own story it is possible that there was more than an author allowing herself to get too fond of one character at the expense of the others, behind her reason for allowing Roberta so large a part of her book. About five years before she wrote *The Railway Children* Nesbit's most dearly loved son, Fabian, had died very unexpectedly after what was an acknowledged minor operation. He was fifteen at the time, and in many ways very like his mother, and her grief when he died, made worse no doubt by shock, had been appalling. She outwardly got over the boy's death and picked up her normal life again, but she never ceased to suffer over Fabian, and whenever she allowed herself to think about him, the wound inflicted by his death split wide open. Was this the reason why, in this purely family book where the drawing of characters counted for so much, she kept a girl always in the foreground; had she drawn Peter as clearly as she drew Roberta, would it have hurt too much?

The Railway Children is an unexpectedly constructed book coming from the pen of E. Nesbit, for in this one book she is full of facts. For instance, she states clearly how old her children are, Roberta has a twelfth birthday, Peter was ten before the family crash, so Phyllis was presumably seven or eight. This may be the reason why the adventures in this book show the children to advantage, for Roberta at

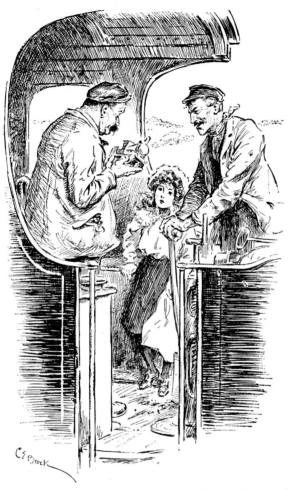

*The engine-driver took the little engine and
looked at it*

THE RAILWAY CHILDREN

A PHOTOGRAPH FROM THE B.B.C.'S TELEVISION
PRODUCTION OF 'THE RAILWAY CHILDREN'

twelve was too old to be allowed to do anything down-right silly, and as Nesbit needed and wanted her in every scene, Peter and Phyllis had to do what Roberta did. Certainly Peter stole the coal, but generally the reasons why the children behave as they do are so admirable in motive, that if the family were drawn less well they could have turned out shocking little prigs. That they do not is also due to the small characters, such as the beautifully written Perks who, by sheer common sense, jerks the children back to normal when too much bravery has made them appear a little too good to be true to life.

In *The Railway Children* E. Nesbit, who through all her children's books makes anything possible if it suits her purpose, introduces something from her own childhood which did not belong to the period about which she was writing. Of course she knew that children in 1905 had never seen a red flannel petti-coat, but did that bother her? Not in the slightest. In the last century there had been red flannel petti-coats, and in her book there were still red flannel pettitcoats, if there were not what else were the chil-dren to tear up to make red flags to stop a train? Excellent reasoning, and who cares that it could not have happened.

It is a pity that E. Nesbit took so much trouble to get rid of her mothers, for when she did draw one she is wholly delightful. Though not in the least like her author in temperament, she was like her in courage; perhaps that is why in many pages in this book Mother's bravery is most moving, for no one knew better than E. Nesbit what it was like to keep smiling, and sound cheerful against what to others seemed hopeless odds. Who that has read *The Railway Children* can forget Mother's entrance into Three

Chimneys? She must, poor woman, have been almost stunned by what had happened to her, and was exhausted by packing, and the long journey, and the walk to the house had been dark and muddy. The house when they reached it was cold, there was the skittering of mice, and matches had to be fumbled for before candles could be lit, so she would have been near to tears, but what did she say?

'You've often wanted something to happen and now it has. This is quite an adventure, isn't it?'

And when there appears to be no waiting meal, as she had hoped, with what gaiety she improvised one from the left-overs from the old home.

'"Bravo!" cried Mother, coming in with a tray full of things. "This is something like!"'

And when the children were in bed, and she was left to tidy up, though she must have been desolate, almost beyond bearing, she called out:

'"Good-night, chickies, I'm sure there aren't any rats. But I'll leave my door open, and then if a mouse comes, you need only scream, and I'll come and tell it exactly what I think of it."'

Had E. Nesbit been alive during the last war, she would have been interested to see how truly she had written that scene, not for one brave mother at the beginning of the century, but for brave mothers everywhere in the nineteen-forties, who knew that security, though non-existent, could be built by words. It might have touched her had she been alive and able to visit a shelter, to watch mothers making home out of a hard bench, and to have heard them, in words very similar to those used by her mother in *The Railway Children*, assuring their offspring that while they were around there was nothing of which to be afraid.

Either because she always intended to, or because she got as fond of Mother as her readers were to be later, E. Nesbit identified herself with 'Mother' in her book sufficiently to insert a little memorial to her own mother, who had died in 1902. She had, as shown from her articles already quoted, adored her mother, who, though an old woman when she died, had remained very close to her daughter. So it was natural when she saw an opportunity for E. Nesbit to insert a few words to show how much she missed her mother.

'"No one," she said at last, "ever loved anyone more than my mother loved me."

'Then she was quiet again, and Bobbie kicked Phyllis hard under the table, because Bobbie understood a little bit the thoughts that were making Mother so quiet – the thoughts of the time when Mother was a little girl and was all the world to *her* mother. It seems so easy and natural to run to Mother when one is in trouble. Bobbie understood a little how people do not leave off running to their mothers when they are in trouble even when they are grown up, and she thought she knew a little what it must be to be sad, and have no mother to run to any more.'

In studying the Nesbit books as a whole *The Railway Children* has perhaps to be considered separately for it stands alone. It has not the brilliance of the Bastable books, nor the blazing imagination of the magic books, but it has that most difficult quality to get on to paper, a solid home life. In this one book E. Nesbit shares qualities with Louisa Alcott, for her Roberta is just as alive as the four *Little Women*, and indeed has something in common with both Jo and

Beth. And though Peter and Phyllis are a little less clearly drawn they are still living children, and by no means mere feeds for Roberta.

Because she made her family so real, it was hard for E. Nesbit to remember they were only figures from her imagination, and that the time must come when she would have finished with them, for she ends her book as if she was following them on tip-toe.

'I think it will be best for us to go quickly and quietly away. At the end of the field, among the thin gold spikes of grass and the harebells and Gipsy roses and St. John's Wort, we may just take one last look, over our shoulders, at the white house where neither we nor anyone else is wanted now.'

Many readers have wished since she wrote those words that she had not been so tactful, but had gone inside, and written more books about the same children. Perhaps sometimes she even wished that herself, for though she was to write of other children, she was never again to know them in the round, as she had known her Railway family.

CHAPTER THIRTEEN

'*The Enchanted Castle*'

IN 1906, the year *The Railway Children* was published, a new story of E. Nesbit's was serialized in *The Strand Magazine*. It was called *The Enchanted Castle*. Nobody but the author knows when, what they are about to write, first takes shape in their brain, so since E. Nesbit is dead any ideas about her books can only be guess-work. When that strange book *The Enchanted Castle* was first conceived, was she planning it while she wrote *The Railway Children*? Studying her work for children as a whole, this seems likely, for though now and again there are passages of great beauty, and in none of her other books does she make the nearness of a magic world to the everyday world so clearly felt, it is difficult not to believe that this book suffered, not so much from being written in a hurry, as from having had the time of thinking about it scamped. Either because she was so fertile of ideas, or because the money tempted her, Nesbit did write books now and then which were not true Nesbit books, and so are best forgotten, and *The Enchanted Castle* might have been a book in that class were it not for the way it blazes into sudden unexpected beauty, and for the only macabre terrifying scenes she ever wrote for children.

In the Robert, Anthea, Jane and Cyril magic books, as already mentioned, E. Nesbit seemed to try by various strategies to keep her public from knowing her children, and she used the same methods in *The Enchanted Castle*; Gerald, Jimmy, Kathleen and Mabel are so shadowy that the magic which the book is about can grip the reader without the distraction of thinking about the human beings. The children with the exception of Mabel have no surnames, and no ages, and no parents that the reader ever meets, for in her usual adroit way E. Nesbit disposes of them on her second page.

'Their Cousin Betty was to be there too, and there were plans. Betty's school broke up before theirs, and so she got to the Hampshire home first, and the moment she got there she began to have measles, so that my three couldn't go home at all.'

Throughout the book Gerald is given some character by the turn of his conversation, which is a pale reflection of Oswald Bastable's:

'"Well, what luck?" the others asked.

'"It's all right," said Gerald indifferently. "I told you it would be. The ingenuous youth won the regard of the foreign governess, who in her youth had been the beauty of her humble village."'

'"How *do* you do it?" Kathleen whispered admiringly as they said good night.

'"Oh, it's quite easy when you've once got a grown-up to see what you're after. You'll see, I shall drive her with a rein of darning cotton after this."'

But at no time is Gerald or any of the other children brought to life or seen, let alone in the round, even in profile, for Nesbit had clearly not lived with the children or thought about them, so they have no past and no future, and are merely cardboard cut-outs on which to hang her magic. This suited her purpose, for she could not have skimmed over what it felt like to be a marble statue, or four yards high, if her children had been real, and that would have meant she would have had a lot of explaining to do about how it felt, and that their author would have had to think out proper answers, which she would have found boring.

Even the most careful study of *The Enchanted Castle* does not give a clear picture of how the magic worked. It was based on a ring and wishes, but there was, as the children knew, far more to it than that. There were, for instance, the marble Gods who did not need the ring, though they understood it. Phoebus tried to explain his particular sort of magic when talking about feasting with the ladies of Olympus.

'"But it won't be real food," urged Mabel.

'"It will be real to you, as to us," said Phoebus; "there is no other realness even in your many-coloured world."'

It is likely that *The Enchanted Castle* came into being, as have many books, as the result of something said or done which fascinates the author, lodges in their brain and refuses to move out. What lodged in Nesbit's brain and refused to move was the Ugly-Wuglies. They were creatures made up of hockey sticks, umbrellas, and broom handles, with paper painted faces, but dressed in real clothes and with stuffed-out gloves on their stick arms. She had used such figures in charades, as who has not, but either her made-up creatures were particularly life-like, or they were new to her, but whatever the reason they stayed with her, leering at her with their painted eyes, and mouthing at her through their painted lips. They

I

must have been to her all the nightmares of her childhood come to roost, and there can be no doubt that
they terrified her, as they were to terrify the children
who read about them. Their impact in a book for
children is the more scarifying in that they alone have
had the full thinking time their author needed to
know them intimately, and so when Eliza the maid
and Mademoiselle saw the creatures for the first time,
sitting at the back of the room as part of the audience
for *Beauty and the Beast*, it was no wonder they
screamed. Eliza said: 'They ain't got no insides', and
then follows this description:

'The seven members of the audience seated among
the wilderness of chairs had, indeed, no insides to
speak of. Their bodies were bolsters and rolled-up
blankets, their spines were broom-handles, and their
arm and leg bones were hockey sticks and umbrellas.
Their shoulders were the wooden cross-pieces that
Mademoiselle used for keeping her jackets in shape;
their hands were gloves stuffed out with handker-
chiefs; and their faces were the paper masks painted
in the afternoon by the untutored brush of Gerald,
tied on to the round heads made of the ends of stuffed
bolster-cases. The faces were really rather dreadful.
Gerald had done his best, but even after his best had
been done you would hardly have known they were
faces, some of them, if they hadn't been in the positions which faces usually occupy, between the collar
and the hat. Their eyebrows were furious with lamp-
black frowns – their eyes the size, and almost the
shape, of five-shilling pieces, and on their lips and
cheeks had been spent much crimson lake and nearly
the whole of a half-pan of vermilion.'
Then Mabel, longing for more applause from the

audience, wished the creatures were alive, and they were.

'Mademoiselle began it: she applauded the garden scene – with hurried little clappings of her quick French hands. Eliza's fat red palms followed heavily, and then – someone else was clapping, six or seven people, and their clapping made a dull padded sound. Nine faces instead of two were turned towards the stage, and seven out of the nine were painted, pointed paper faces. And every hand and every face was alive.'

It must have been while Nesbit was brooding on that horrid muffled clapping, and was frightening herself by it, that she knew how the creatures talked. Their mouths were mere slits in the paper, so they could have no roofs to them, so they should talk in the slow way of those whose mouths are misformed. '"Aa oo ré o me me oo a oo ho el?" said the voice again. And it had said it four times before Gerald could collect himself sufficiently to understand that this horror – alive, and most likely quite uncontrollable – was saying, with a dreadful calm, polite persistence:—

'"Can you recommend me to a good hotel?"'

It could only be that E. Nesbit had become herself a frightened child again that allowed her to write the scenes that followed, for nowhere else does she set out to terrify children. The truth was the Ugly-Wuglies had got hold of her pen and refused to let go of it. Pattering along in dreadful procession, mouthing their requests for a lodging if not a hotel, asking why carriages had not been ordered to take them home, the paper creatures with no insides and umbrella arms grow more and more human in an evil way. All robots have a frightening quality about them, but

Nesbit's creatures made of odds and ends become positively revolting.

'The respectable Ugly-Wugly leading with the lamp, the others following trustfully, one and all disappeared into that narrow doorway; and Gerald and Mabel standing without, hardly daring to breathe lest a breath should retard the procession, almost sobbed with relief. Prematurely, as it turned out. For suddenly there was a rush and a scuffle inside the passage, and as they strove to close the door the Ugly-Wuglies fiercely pressed to open it again. Whether they saw something in the dark passage that alarmed them, whether they took it into their empty heads that this could not be the back way to any really respectable hotel, or whether a convincing sudden instinct warned them that they were being tricked, Mabel and Gerald never knew. But they knew that the Ugly-Wuglies were no longer friendly and commonplace, that a fierce change had come over them. Cries of "No, No!" "We won't go on!" "Make *him* lead!" broke the dreamy stillness of the perfect night. There were screams from ladies' voices, the hoarse, determined shouts of strong Ugly-Wuglies roused to resistance, and, worse than all, the steady pushing open of that narrow stone door that had almost closed upon the ghastly crew. Through the chink of it they could be seen, a writhing black crowd against the light of the bicycle lamp; a padded hand reached round the door; stick-boned arms stretched out angrily towards the world that that door, if it closed, would shut them off from for ever. And the tone of their consonantless speech was no longer conciliatory and ordinary; it was threatening, full of the menace of unbearable horrors.'

The children escaped unhurt, but the owner of The

Castle, who came to help shut the door, was later found unconscious, gashed on the forehead by an Ugly-Wugly. To allow that sort of occurrence was again so unlike Nesbit it was as if she was possessed. Why otherwise should she who knew only too well the fears of childhood, deliberately introduce her readers to a new one? All children have at some time dressed up an inanimate object and pretended it was alive, but it is understood when the game is over the object returns to its proper use, though scared children have said: 'I've stopped playing but it won't stop pretending.' But E. Nesbit with her Ugly-Wuglies did worse than that, the creatures not only went on pretending long after the game had finished, but could go on playing when the children were not there, and were able in their absence to inflict real bodily harm. A terrifying idea to hand to an imaginative child.

Against the strange background of her Ugly-Wuglies is some real magic, the sort that did not need a Psammead, a carpet, a Phoenix, an Amulet, or a ring, the magic that lies within the reach of everyone who has the courage to lean against the invisible wall that hides it.

'There is a curtain, thin as gossamer, clear as glass, strong as iron, that hangs for ever between the world of magic and the world that seems to us to be real. And when once people have found one of the little weak spots in that curtain which are marked by magic rings, and amulets, and the like, almost anything may happen.

'The moonbeam slants more and more; now it touches the far end of the stone, now it draws nearer and nearer to the middle of it, now at last it touches the very heart and centre of that central stone. And then it is as though a spring were touched, a fountain of light released. Everything changes. Or, rather, everything is revealed. There are no more secrets. The plan of the world seems plain, like an easy sum that one writes in big figures on a child's slate. One wonders how one can ever have wondered about anything. Space is not; every place that one has seen or dreamed of is here. Time is not; into this instant is crowded all that one has ever done or dreamed of doing. It is a moment, and it is eternity. It is the centre of the universe and it is the universe itself. The eternal light rests on and illuminates the eternal heart of things.'

A queer strange book *The Enchanted Castle.*

*She saw that fully half of the chairs were occupied
and by the queerest people*

THE ENCHANTED CASTLE

The Mouldiwarp made a little run and a little jump

THE HOUSE OF ARDEN

CHAPTER FOURTEEN

'The House of Arden' and 'Harding's Luck'

OF ALL the books that E. Nesbit wrote for children, the most puzzling to a searcher into how they were conceived are *The House of Arden* and *Harding's Luck*. On the known facts *The House of Arden* was written first, it was published in 1908; *Harding's Luck* was serialised a year later. In actual fact the books were probably written at the same time, and certainly were brooded over in Nesbit's mind at the same time, and it is possible that *Harding's Luck* was conceived first, which would account for some odd goings on in *The House of Arden*, and for the really brutal treatment the author handed out to Edred, the boy in that story.

The two books cannot be taken apart, for on a number of occasions in *Harding's Luck* E. Nesbit merely states that this or that has already been described in *The House of Arden*. In *The House of Arden* the two children, Edred aged ten and Elfrida aged twelve, are mere outlines of children. They had no parents, though their father was expected back from South America where he had been prospecting. But of course with magic in the offing E. Nesbit did not want a father hanging about, so he and an uncle who was with him were conveniently captured and supposedly killed by brigands. This left only an aunt, a Miss Arden, in whose lodging house the children live. And even the aunt was rapidly disposed of, because when Edred inherits Arden Castle the aunt is left behind for the whole book trying to let the lodging-house.

The magic creature in *Harding's Luck* is the Mouldiwarp. Perhaps carried away by the various forms of magic she had used in *The Enchanted Castle*, the Mouldiwarp is not nearly so cut and dried a character as either the Psammead or the Phoenix. Those two miraculous creatures knew exactly where their powers began and ended and what they would, or more often in the case of the Psammead, would not, do. Life was not nearly so easy for the Mouldiwarp, who could be got at in various ways. Officially the beast was the badge of Arden House, and if called by verse, could come to the assistance of an Arden, and it could grant wishes, but it had duties which the Psammead and the Phoenix had not, and this duty was to make the new Lord Arden brave, kind and wise, and as well eventually to show him where the treasure was hidden.

This story, when E. Nesbit was thinking it out, probably sounded fine, but in the working out it was tough on Edred, and even tougher on the Mouldiwarp. The Psammead and the Phoenix had been outspoken, but they had never had to improve anybody, and here was the Mouldiwarp wedded to the job. In order to carry out the brave, kind and wise part of his commission, the Mouldiwarp refused to help Edred to visit the Past, unless he and Elfrida had been nice to each other for a whole day. This was a disaster and E. Nesbit quickly sickened of it. Children living in the country in an unexplored castle, who find it difficult not to quarrel for even one day are a bore, and a bore she made them, and a bore the Mouldiwarp found them. So then E. Nesbit turned her attention to her unwritten book *Harding's Luck*, and focused everyone's attention on Cousin Richard of that story, a boy who seemed to belong to the Past, of whom the Mouldiwarp says admiringly:

'"Ah!" . . . "he be summat like an Arden, he be."'

It is curious, seeing that the two books are interlocked and that the children in both are Ardens, that E. Nesbit concocted different kinds of magic for each. In *The House of Arden*, apart from calling for the Mouldiwarp, almost no form of magic is barred: swans made of snow and snow coats, magic clocks, visions, and a witch are amongst the means of transportation used. In *Harding's Luck* Richard gets into the Past by making a real old magic sign, in flower seeds, and though he uses Edred and Elfrida's magic on occasion, his own remains simple and the easiest to understand.

The first half of *Harding's Luck* has some of the best Nesbit story-telling; that the whole book is not one of her finest is because it has to be patchy owing to the fact that she had already told a large part of the story in *The House of Arden*. How soon in the writing of *The House of Arden* was she absorbed by Richard? It is a fascinating idea, the cripple boy known as Dickie Harding from Deptford, who takes to the road with a tramp called Beale, and there learns to beg and almost to be a thief. Then by his magic triangles he slips into the Past, where he is not lame and is the son of well-to-do Sir Richard Arden. Dickie's magic is so cut and dried that he knows that he can slip into the Past at any time where he will not be lame, and will be rich, but fondness for Beale the tramp always drags him back. Yet when the boy goes back for good, as he does, it was not because he wanted to, but because he felt he was taking too much from others if he stayed in his own century.

No wonder, having thought up this splendid plot which is full of excitement both in the Past and in the present, E. Nesbit longed to start writing her story, and so had not much time for quarrelsome Edred, who was taking so long to become brave and good and wise. In fact, towards the end of *The House of Arden* she got so out of patience with him that she was always finding ways to get rid of him, just as in most of her books she got rid of parents:

'I should like to tell you also what happened to Edred, but his part of the adventure was not really an adventure at all – though it was a thing that he will never forget as long as he remembers any magic happenings.'

Almost certainly, though she allowed Edred to improve by the end of *Harding's Luck*, she never got to like the boy, and gave the Mouldiwarp, speaking for her, every opportunity to criticize him.

The House of Arden is the only one of the Nesbit children's books in which she, who was one of the original members of The Fabian Society, allows herself to speak her mind on the conditions of her day. In her early children's books it is impossible to believe that she and her husband were devoted to the working classes, for she writes of them, especially of their children, as if they were untouchables, as indeed they almost were to the Bastables, and to Robert, Anthea, Jane and Cyril. But in *The House of Arden* she had an opportunity to let Dickie speak for her. It was when the three children were comparing their day, with life in the reign of Henry VIII, in which they were then living, and Edred said:

'"They don't cut your head off for nothing anyhow in our times, and shut you up in the Tower."

'"They do worse things," Richard said. "*I* know. They make people work fourteen hours a day for nine shillings a week, so that they never have enough to eat or wear, and no time to sleep or to be happy in. They won't give people food or clothes, or let them work to get them; and then they put the people in prison if they take enough to keep them alive. They let people get horrid diseases, till their jaws drop off, so as to have a particular kind of china. Women have to go out to work instead of looking after their babies, and the little girl that's left in charge drops the baby and it's crippled for life. Oh! I know. I won't go back with you. You might keep me there for ever." He shuddered.

'"I wouldn't. And I can't help about people working, and not enough money and that," said Edred.

'"If *I* were Lord Arden," said Richard, through the darkness, "I'd make a vow, and I'd keep it too, never to have a day's holiday or do a single thing I liked till all those things were stopped. But in *your* time nobody cares."'

It was unfair, of course, for Dickie or Richard, as he was called at that date, was comparing life in a Deptford back street with life in court circles, but it was interesting that E. Nesbit allowed herself that outburst, for there had been chances in her other books, and she had not taken them.

Because both the Psammead and the Phoenix had chapters to themselves, it seems only fair that the Mouldiwarp should have his, but he had relations which as far as is known the Psammead and the Phoenix had not. A queer trinity these Warps, hard to understand, but deserving of study.

CHAPTER FIFTEEN

The Warps; Mouldi –
Mouldier – Mouldiest

THE MOULDIWARP was the only member of his family who had to work in a mundane way. In *The House of Arden* he was as busy, and as put out by the calls on his time, as the Psammead. Like the Psammead he had no pretensions to looks, though probably again like the Psammead, he would have disowned such an assertion. It is true when first Edred and Elfrida saw him he appeared to 'glitter goldenly', but that was in the 'pink, diffused light of the sun-setting'. But when 'the last bit of sun dipped behind the shoulder of the downs', though he was the Arden crest, come alive, he was also just a mole, though a white one.

The Mouldiwarp, inconveniently for its author, whose only settled homes both as a child, and as an adult, had been in Kent, was a Sussex animal. Sussex, even if you are born and bred there, is a difficult dialect to catch, and words are hard to pick up, for what is common in one part of Sussex may not be used in another, so it is understandable that the Mouldiwarp did not always speak in dialect, and when he did often used that strange language known in theatrical circles as 'Mummersetshire'. But who is to say the Sussex as spoken by the Mouldiwarp was not very good Sussex in its day, for his day had been a long one, not as long as those of the Psammead or the Phoenix, but the Mouldiwarp had served an old family, for there had been sixteen Lord Ardens, and that was not the beginning according to old Beale – Beale the tramp's father.

'You see the Ardens was always great gentry. I've heard say there's always been Ardens here since before William the Conker, whoever *he* was.'

So, as the Mouldiwarp pushed its way up through the chalk of the Sussex Downs to answer a call from a new Lord Arden, it was understandable that on its tongue was the burr of a very old Sussex indeed, at least that could be the explanation of the way it used the language.

The Mouldiwarp, like Nesbit's other creatures, was outspoken from the first, but, unlike the other two who knew their place was the Past, it belonged to the present, and supposed its calls to the human world to be merely dreams.

'"Don't you tell me," said the Mouldiwarp, bristling a little. "Hasn't no no one told you e'er a fairy tale? All us beastes has tongues, and when we're dere us uses of en."

'"When you're where?' said Edred, rather annoyed at being forced to believe in fairy tales, which he had never really liked.

'"Why, in a fairy tale for sure," said the mole. "Where-ever to goodness else on earth do you suppose you be?"'

In *The House of Arden* E. Nesbit returned to her Bastable pleasure, in making children try to write verse. Unlike Noël Bastable, Elfrida and Edred had no creative urge, they tried to write rhymes only because it was the means of summoning the Mouldiwarp.

'"I've *got* to let you find me again. Don't upset yourself," it said bitterly. "When you wants me, come up on to the knoll and say a piece of poetry to call me, and I'll come."

'"But what poetry?" Edred asked.

'"Oh, anything. You can pick and choose."

'Edred thought of "The Layes of Ancient Rome".

'"Only 'tain't no good without you makes it up yourselves," said the Mouldiwarp.

'"Oh!" said the two, much disheartened.

'"And course it must be askin' me to kindly come to you. Get along home."

'"Where are *you* going?" Elfrida asked. "Home too, of course," it said, and this time it really *did* go.'

The Mouldiwarp had evidently made a deep study of all that rhymed from real poetry to the sort of rhyme that might be found in a Christmas cracker, for it could not be fooled, not even when the words were changed about a bit.

> 'Mole, mole,
> Come out of your hole;
> I know you're blind,
> But *I* don't mind.'

Edred recited and then when the Mouldiwarp did not appear, had to admit the real verse was:

> 'The mole, the mole,
> He lives in a hole.
> The mole is blind;
> *I* don't mind.'

The creature was a critic, for when forced to appear because Edred had recited some very poor verse of

Elfrida's, and had followed it by 'If you don't mind', it said on arrival:

'" . . . call that poetry?"'

Like the Psammead the Mouldiwarp kept its dignity by pretending it was only granting wishes as a favour.

'"What time you'd like to go back to. If you don't choose before I've counted ten it's all off. One two, three, four . . ."'

But when it reached ten and the children had not chosen the period in history they wished to visit, how neatly it changed its tune. It never mentioned that the journey into the Past was not off, but merely said as if it was what was intended all the time:

'"Oh, very well, den you'll have to take your luck, that's all."'

As with all Nesbit's creatures, the Mouldiwarp was educated.

'"Sussex barn an' bred," said the mole, "but I know other talk. Sussex talks what they call 'racy of the soil'– means 'smells of the earth' where I live. I can talk all sorts, though. I used to spit French once on a time, young Fitz-le-seigneur."'

But it usually preferred rustic talk, as for instance when Edred asked it how old it was.

'"'s old as my tongue an' a little older'n me teeth."'

It is hard to get as fond of the Mouldiwarp as of the Psammead or Phoenix, because the truth is it is overshadowed by those superb creations. It could have been as endearing in its own way, and likely enough when its author was giving it birth it seemed as if it would become equally outstanding, but it never turned out to be, and almost certainly the reason is the stories which encumber it. Robert, Anthea, Jane and Cyril may not have been very interesting children, but what happened to them with the Psammead and the Phoenix, assisted by the carpet and the Amulet, was perfectly understandable. In *Five Children and It* the Psammead, however unwillingly, could and did grant wishes. In *The Phoenix and the Carpet*, the carpet with much advice from the Phoenix, who on occasion asked advice from the Psammead, could and did transport the children wherever they wanted to go. In *The Story of the Amulet*, on the Word of Power the children could pass into the Past, and the Psammead strictly adhered to the no-wishes-for-the-family ruling laid down at the end of *Five Children and It*. But in *The House of Arden,* and in *Harding's Luck,* the Mouldiwarp is deprived of clear-cut magic functions, in fact swamped by too much unaccounted for magic it dwindles, and dwindles, until its personality is a mere flicker. It is a tragedy, for at the beginning of the book it seemed to have the makings of as fine a creature as his famous predecessors.

The Mouldiwarp's powers begin to diminish in 1605, when the children's nurse of that date, who was really a witch, called it by a new and incorrect method.

'She breathed on the salver and traced triangles and a circle on the drilled surface; and as the mistiness of her breath faded and the silver shone out again un-dimmed, there, suddenly, in the middle of the salver, was the live white Mouldiwarp of Arden, looking extremely cross!

'"You've no manners," it said to the nurse, "bring-ing me here in that offhand, rude way, without 'With your leave', or 'By your leave!' Elfrida could easily have made some poetry. You know well enough," it added angrily, "that it's positively painful to me to be summoned by your triangles and things. Poetry's so easy and simple."

"'Poetry's too slow for this night's work," said the nurse shortly. "Come, take the children away, I have done with it."

"'You make everything so difficult," said the Mouldiwarp, more crossly than ever. "That's the worse of people who think they know a lot and really only know a little, and pretend they know everything. If I'd come the easy poetry way, I could have taken them back as easily. But now . . . Well, it can't be helped. I'll take them back, of course, but it'll be a way they won't like. They'll have to go on to the top of the roof and jump off."'

Puzzling for any child, and it is hard to see why Nesbit wrote that scene, as the Mouldiwarp itself says the children could have got back the easy poetry way. But having allowed Edred and Elfrida one sort of magic, and Dickie Harding another, she no doubt felt that this was the moment to join the two together, so she allowed the nurse to draw Dickie's triangles, and made them bring the Mouldiwarp. But why did she write what followed next, when the children, it will be remembered, had to jump from a top floor window into space?

"'I mean you're to jump out right enough," said the Mouldiwarp. "What you're to jump into's any pair of shoes – and it's my look-out, anyway."'

And when they did jump why were they not back in the present, why did they find themselves in a snow carriage, drawn by snow swans? E. Nesbit had to make Edred brave and jumping out of a window was a courageous thing to do, but it did lower the

K

Mouldiwarp's dignity, and it is almost possible to hear the Psammead say 'There was none of that sort of nonsense in the good old Megatherium days'.

The swan carriage adds to the puzzling situation by carrying the children to Arden Castle as it was when it was first built, and there they experience other kinds of magic in which the Mouldiwarp has no part, the snow fur coats belong here, and so does magic washing arrangements.

'Elfrida jumped up and threw off the silver-white, downy-soft coverlet. It instantly tore itself into five pieces of different shapes and sizes, and these screwed themeelves up, and drew themselves in, and blew themselves out, and turned before her very eyes into a silver basin of warm water, a piece of lily-scented soap, a towel, a silver comb, and an ivory toothbrush.'

But the final insult to the Mouldiwarp was in the manner in which the children eventually got home. Very properly, the situation being serious, Elfrida made up some poetry, but did the Mouldiwarp appear as in duty bound it was forced to do, not at all.

'And the moment she had said it, the white magic coats grew up and grew down and wrapped the children up as tight and as soft as ever a silkworm wrapped itself when it was tired of being a silkworm and entered into its cocoon, as the first step towards being a person with wings.

'Can you imagine what it would be like to have lovely liquid sleep emptied on you by the warm tubful? That is what it felt like inside the white, wonderful cocoons. The children knew that the tower was turning wrong way up and inside out, but it didn't matter a bit. Sleep was raining down on them in magic

showers – no; it was closing on them, closer and
closer, nearer and nearer, soft, delicious layers of
warm delight. A soft, humming sound was in their
ears, like the sound of bees when you push through a
bed of Canterbury bells, and the next thing that
happened was that they came out of the past into the
present with a sort of snap of light and a twist of
sound. It was like coming out of a railway tunnel
into daylight.

'The magic coverlet-coat-cocoons had even saved
them the trouble of changing into their own clothes,
for they found that the stiff, heavy clothes had gone,
and they were dressed in the little ordinary things
that they had always been used to.'

It is beyond understanding how E. Nesbit thought
that up, beautifully written though it is, for to her
readers, as she very well knew, rules were rules, and
when poetry was invented, and said, the Mouldiwarp
had to appear.

Towards the end of *The House of Arden* it seems as
if E. Nesbit had read through her book as far as it
went and suddenly realised what she had done to her
Mouldiwarp, for when she is off on what Edred un-
gratefully, but properly described as '*more* magic', and
he did not say it politely – she wrote this paragraph:

'I think myself that the white Mouldiwarp was
anxious to help a little. I believe it had arranged the
whole of this exhibition so that the children might
get an idea of the whereabouts of the treasure, and so
cease to call on it at all hours of the day and night
with the sort of poetry which even a mole must see
not to be so *very* good.'

It was a half-hearted sort of explanation for she

knew, as all writers know when they have done it, that she had neglected her own character, and in her case in so doing had mishandled the extraordinary gift that Heaven had given her. As if to atone for a page or two after that she brought the Mouldiwarp back.

"'Tch, tch!" said the mole, rubbing its nose with vexation. "There's another chance gone, and gone for ever. You be terrible spending with your chances, you be. Now, answer sharp as weasel's nose. Be there any one in the past you'd like to see?"

> "'If you don't know,
> Then you don't go."

"'And that's poetry as good as yours any day of the week."'

But in the last chapter of *The House of Arden* she let it down again, forcing it to take a new shape, something the Psammead and the Phoenix would have refused to permit their author to do to them. It was all because of another new kind of magic. This time it was getting through a crack in the ground, where there was a fancy clock which held time steady, of which she had become fond. Edred had demanded to be taken to where his father was, and suddenly there was the Mouldiwarp travelling with them, but this time 'the size of an enormous Polar bear'.

In *Harding's Luck* the Mouldiwarp does not appear until the latter part of the book, for it is of course Dickie's story and the Mouldiwarp was not Dickie's sort of magic. It was the witch-nurse who told Dickie about it.

"'. . . but can't *I* see the white Mouldiwarp?"
"'I dare not – even *I* dare not call it again tonight,"

the nurse owned. "But maybe I will teach thee a little spell to bring it on another day. It is an angry little beast at times, but kindly and hard-working."'

Then the nurse made this surprising statement.

'"There are three white Mouldiwarps friends to thy house," she told him –"the Mouldiwarp who is the badge, and the Mouldiwarp who is the crest, and the Great Mouldiwarp who sits on the green and white chequered field of the Ardens' shield of arms."'

It is almost certain the Mouldiwarp had no relations when first Nesbit conceived it. Why then did she make it part of a trinity? The answer must be that she never should in the first place have given Dickie different magic from that used by Edred and Elfrida, they were all Ardens and as such should have been served by the same mole. She was perhaps in a hurry, for she had many commitments outside her books for children, and indeed re-writing those parts of *The House of Arden*, which concerned Dickie, would have been a big undertaking, so she thought up the two other Warps. It was not a satisfactory solution, for it gave a mystical quality to the Warps, which injured what was left of the personality of the gruff, tough, Sussex born Mouldiwarp. But at the very end of *Harding's Luck* the real Mouldiwarp is allowed to reappear for a moment. Dickie was desperate, because he had led his cousins into trouble with the Roundheads, and could see no way by which he could get out of prison to help them.

'"Bide where you be, lad, bide still; "tis only me – old Mouldiwarp of Arden. You be a bold lad, by my faith, so you be. Never an Arden better. Never an Arden of them all."

'"Oh, Mouldiwarp, dear Mouldiwarp, do help me! I led them into this – help me to get them back safe. Do, do, do!"

'"So I will, den – dere ain't no reason in getting all of a fluster. It ain't fitten for a lad as 'as faced death same's what you 'ave," said the voice. "I've made a liddle tunnel for 'e – so I 'ave – 'ere in dis 'ere corner – you come caten wise crose the floor and you'll feel it."'

It was the Mouldiwarp's last appearance, but a good one, for though it was not part of its usual magic what could be a more suitable occupation for a mole than to make 'a liddle tunnel'?

Though the Mouldiwarp was never allowed to rise to the stature of E. Nesbit's other two creatures, it is still an outstanding figure in children's fiction. In criticising even mildly, it is not that the two Mouldiwarp books are not good, they are, but it was in the magician's power to make them so much better.

CHAPTER SIXTEEN

The Magician

WHAT A surprise it would have been to the child
E. Nesbit who first went to live at The Hall at Halstead if she could have seen her future. All of us when
we were children dreamed dreams about what we
would be and do when we grew up, and for many this
meant a new dream every year. But for the child
Nesbit there were no changes of heart, she was to
be a poet, that was a certainty. She wrote of that
time:

'. . . I had a little room of my own, a little, little
room, with a long low window and a window-ledge,
where bright plants in pots, encouraged by the west-
ern sun, withstood the intermittence of my attentions,
and blossomed profusely. My bookcase stood by this
window, an old mahogany bookcase with a deep top
drawer, that let down to form a writing-table. Here I
used to sit and write – verse, verse, always verse –
and dream of the days when I should be a great poet,
like Shakespeare, or Christina Rossetti! But I never
doubted then that it would come.'

If that child, dreaming in her room of her future
as a poet, could come back, would she mind that her
fame rests on work so different? Probably at the age
about which she was writing the answer would be yes,

she would have minded, for in the teens to want something is to want it very badly indeed. But would the E. Nesbit who died in 1924 have cared? That is something nobody, even those closest to her could answer. The work of all creative artists falls pitiably short of their vision, but only they know what was the vision. Thinking of all that she had written in her lifetime, was E. Nesbit disappointed with her achievement, did she sometimes grudge E. Nesbit the author of the children's books the laurel wreath she wished could have been won by E. Nesbit the poet, or, failing that by E. Nesbit the novelist? The answer to that question went to the grave with her.

What is known is the respect with which her children's books were received during her lifetime by her fellow writers. Her position in the literary world is hard to understand today, for there is no living writer for children who holds anything approaching the position she held. Letters from the distinguished flowed in on her, and towards the end of her life admirers made pilgrimages to visit her, something it is impossible to imagine happening even to her today. Perhaps the second world war has left such a life behind it, adult writers have no time to consider books for children seriously, and indeed there are precious few living writers for children who deserve such consideration. But for Nesbit the appreciation her work received must have been a consolation for any disappointment she may have felt in the reception of her work for adults, but did it compensate for her knowledge that her poetry would be forgotten?

In the last article she wrote for *The Girl's Own Paper*, she describes in prose and poetry the Kent she knew and loved.

'Oh, those dewy mornings – the resurrection of light and life in the woods and fields! Would that it were possible for all children to live in the country where they may drink in, consciously or unconsciously, the dear delights of green meadow and dappled woodland! The delight in green things growing, in the tender beauty of the evening light on grey pastures, the glorious splendour of the noonday sun on meadows golden with buttercups, the browns and purples of winter woodlands – this is a delight that grows with one's growth – a delight that "age cannot wither nor custom stale", a delight that the years who take from us so much can never take away – can but intensify and make more keen and precious.

'Nature never did betray
The heart that loved her.'

'My book of memory lies open always at the page where are the pictures of Kentish cherry orchards, field and farm and gold-dim woodlands starred with primroses, light copses where the bluebells and wind-flowers grow. Yes, bluebells and wind-flowers to me and to all who love them. Botanists who pull the poor, pretty things to pieces may call them hyacinths and anemones.

'And most plainly of all, among the dream pictures shows our old garden at home.

'There is a grey-walled garden far away
    From noise and smoke of cities where the hours
    Pass with soft wings among the happy flowers
And lovely leisure blossoms every day.

'There, tall and white, the sceptral lily blows;
    There grow the pansy pink and columbine,
    Brave holly-hocks and star-white jessamine
And the red glory of the royal rose.

'There greeny glow-worms gem the dusky lawn,
  The lime-trees breathe their fragrance to the night,
  Pink roses sleep, and dream that they are white
Until they wake to colour with the dawn.

'There in the splendour of the sultry noon
  The sunshine sleeps upon the garden bed,
  Where the white poppy droops a drowsy head
And dreams of kisses from the white full moon.

        ...   .

'And there, all day, my heart goes wandering,
  Because there first my heart began to know
  The glories of the summer and the snow,
The loveliness of harvest and of spring.

'There may be fairer gardens – but I know
  There is no other garden half so dear
  Because 'tis there, this many, many a year,
The sacred sweet white flowers of memory grow.'

As she wrote this did she think about those children she had created to whom she had denied even a
smell of the country? Why did E. Nesbit, who so
worshipped country life and who felt a town child
was a deprived child, deliberately choose town set-
tings for the first families she created? Why did the
Bastables have to live in a semi-detached house in
Lewisham, and even when they were well-off, only
get as far as Blackheath? Why did Robert, Anthea,
Jane, Cyril and the Lamb live in Camden Town, and
though it is true in *Five Children and It* they were in
The White House on the edge of a hill, most of their
lives were spent in London, including those months in
Old Nurse's lodgings near the British Museum? The
answer is a key to the Nesbit magic, that early, so
vividly remembered childhood in Kennington Lane.
Although she never brought children so excitingly to

life as she did in *The Railway Children,* that book is
an exception in that its roots were planted in her
early married life, but taking her work as a whole it
is true to write of her that she was at her best when
she wrote from her memory of her own childhood.
No one can write always of their best, but what a
superb best hers was.

After E. Nesbit died in May 1924, C. L. Graves
wrote these verses for *Punch,* which sum up E. Nesbit's place in the children's book shelves:

IN MEMORIAM – E. NESBIT
(Neminem tristem fecit – Old Latin Epitaph)

> E. Nesbit – what unclouded joys
>   That name, familiar on the cover
> Of twenty books for girls and boys
>   Recalls to every story-lover!
>
> You flattered both the old and young
>   In your exhilarating pages,
> Enhancing with a golden tongue
>   All that is charming in all ages.
>
> How we adored *The Would-be-Goods*
>   And drank delight in brimming beakers
> Exploring likely neighbourhoods
>   For treasure with the *Treasure-Seekers!*
>
> Would that your *Bastables* could be
>   Indefinitely duplicated,
> So rare in life, it is to see
>   High spirits with good manners mated.
>
> Later you spread, each Christmas time,
>   Your magic mat for every corner,
> And bore us smoothly to the clime
>   Of Wonderland and endless summer.

With you in elfin halls we drained
  Nectar from jewelled fairy flagons,
Most amiably entertained
  By friendly Phoenixes and Dragons.

You waved your wand, and swift upsprang
  Enchanted castles, magic cities;
You were a poetess, and sang
  Delectable fantastic ditties.

          ...   .

You pass, but only from the ken
  Of scientists and statisticians,
To join HANS CHRISTIAN ANDERSEN,
  The Prince of all the good Magicians.

So, for the joyance that you gave,
  Inspired by love, not code or system,
Punch lays his laurel on your grave,
  Quod neminem fecisti tristem.

E. Nesbit (1858-1924)

A LIST OF HER CHILDREN'S BOOKS

The accompanying list of E. Nesbit's books for children is arranged chronologically in accordance with the first appearance of the various titles; it includes brief bibliographical details of the first edition of each, together with particulars of the latest editions of those which have been re-issued and are available to-day. It makes no claim to absolute completeness, having been compiled from such records as the publishers were able to obtain from the ordinary recognised sources. Admirers of Nesbit may well be in possession of other information which has not come to light; and the publishers would greatly value any such information which might help to establish a complete Nesbit Juvenile Bibliography.

Some Tales in Collections [*Raphael Tuck & Son*]   1894

As Happy as a King. *Illustrated by* s. ROSAMUND PRAEGER [*Marcus Ward & Co.*]   1896

The Children's Shakespeare. *Edited by* EDRIC VREDENBURG [*Raphael Tuck & Son*]   1897

Tales Told in the Twilight. *By* E. NESBIT, O. MOLESWORTH and others [*Raphael Tuck & Son*]   1897

Royal Children of English History
                    [*Raphael Tuck & Son*]   1897

The Story of the Treasure Seekers. *Illustrated by*
   GORDON BROWNE *and* LEWIS BAUMER
                  [*T. Fisher Unwin*] 1899

   Reset edition with original illustrations
                  [*Ernest Benn*] 1958

The Book of Dragons. *Illustrated by* H. R. MILLAR
   with decorations by H. GRANVILLE FELL
                  [*Harper Bros.*] 1900

Nine Unlikely Tales for Children. *Illustrated by* H. R.
   MILLAR *and* JEFFESON [*T. Fisher Unwin*] 1901

   Latest impression [*Ernest Benn*] 1938

The Wouldbegoods. *Illustrated by* ARTHUR H. BUCK-
   LAND and others [*T. Fisher Unwin*] 1901

   Reset edition with original illustrations
                  [*Ernest Benn*] 1958

Five Children and It. *Illustrated by* H. R. MILLAR
                [*T. Fisher Unwin*] 1902

   Reset edition with original illustrations
                  [*Ernest Benn*] 1957

The Revolt of the Toys or What Comes of Quarrelling
   (*Two stories*). *Illustrated by* AMBROSE DUDLEY
                  [*Ernest Nisser*] 1902

The Rainbow Queen and Other Stories. *Illustrated
   by* E. *and* N. R. TAYLOR, M. BOWLEY, *etc.*
             [*Raphael Tuck & Son*] 1903

The Phoenix and the Carpet. *Illustrated by* H. R.
   MILLAR [*George Newnes*] 1904

   Facsimile of first edition [*Ernest Benn*] 1956

New Treasure Seekers. *Illustrated by* GORDON BROWNE
   and LEWIS BAUMER [*T. Fisher Unwin*] 1904

   Reset edition. *Illustrated by* C. WALTER HODGES
                  [*Ernest Benn*] 1949

Oswald Bastable and Others. *Illustrated by* C. E.
   BROCK *and* H. R. MILLAR
           [*Wells, Gardner, Darton & Co*] 1905

The Story of the Amulet. *Illustrated by* H. R. MILLAR
[*T. Fisher Unwin*]   1906

   Reset edition with original illustrations
[*Ernest Benn*]   1957

The Enchanted Castle. *Illustrated by* H. R. MILLAR
[*T. Fisher Unwin*]   1907

   Facsimile of first edition [*Ernest Benn*]   1956

The Railway Children. *Illustrated by* C. E. BROCK
[*Wells, Gardner, Darton & Co.*]   1908

   Reset edition. *Illustrated by* LYNTON LAMB
[*Ernest Benn*]   1957

The Old Nursery Stories (No. 1 of the Children's
Bookcase series). *Illustrated by* W. H. MARGETSON,
Edited by E. NESBIT [*Henry Frowde* and
Hodder & Stoughton]   1908–11

The House of Arden. *Illustrated by* H. R. MILLAR
[*T. Fisher Unwin*]   1908

   Reset edition. *Illustrated by* DESMOND E.
WALDUCK [*Ernest Benn*]   1949

These Little Ones. *Illustrated by* SPENCER PRYSE
[*George Allen & Sons*]   1909

Harding's Luck. *Illustrated by* H.R. MILLAR
[*Hodder & Stoughton*]   1909

   Reset edition. *Illustrated by* DESMOND E. WALDUCK
[*Ernest Benn*]   1949

The Magic City. *Illustrated by* H. R. MILLAR
[*Macmillan & Co.*]   1910

   Latest impression [*Ernest Benn*]   1958

My Sea-side Story Book (with G. MANVILLE FENN),
Illustrated by W. RAINEY, A. WEBB and others
[*Ernest Nister*]   1911

The Wonderful Garden, or The Three C's. *Illustrated
by* H. R. MILLAR [*Macmillan & Co.*]   1911

   New edition [*Ernest Benn*]   1947

The Magic World. *Illustrated by* H. R. MILLAR *and*
SPENCER PRYSE [*Macmillan & Co.*]　　　　　　1912

New Edition [*Ernest Benn*]　　　　　　　　　　1932

Wet Magic. *Illustrated by* H. R. MILLAR
[*T. Werner Laurie*]　1913

Latest impression [*Ernest Benn*]　　　　　　1958

Our New Story Book, *by* E. NESBIT, MARY BOYLE,
G. R. GLASGOW, CLIFTON BINGHAM and others.
Illustrated by ELSIE WOOD, LOUIS WAIN and others
[*Ernest Nister* and *E. P. Dutton*]　1913

Five of Us—and Madeline. *Illustrated by* NORAH S.
UNWIN [*T. Fisher Unwin*]　　　　　　　　　1925

Reset edition. *Illustrated by* PETER FREEMAN
[*Ernest Benn*]　1958

Complete History of the Bastable Family. *Illustrated by* H. R. MILLAR and others [*Ernest Benn*]　1928

*Printed in Great Britain by Wyman & Sons Ltd.
London, Fakenham and Reading.*